CW00956852

DRAWING THE MERC WITH A MOUTH

DEADPOOL

DRAWING THE MERC WITH A MOUTH

THREE DECADES OF AMAZING MARVEL COMICS ART

MATTHEW K. MANNING

TITAN BOOKS

London

An Insight Editions Book

CONTENTS

INTRODUCTION

He's the Merc with a Mouth—the infamous killer for hire known as Deadpool. The product of genetic experiments carried out by the clandestine Weapon X operation, Deadpool is Marvel's main mercenary, a comic book character unafraid to break the so-called fourth wall and talk directly to his readers. With a wit to rival Spider-Man's and an uncanny healing factor equal to—if not more powerful than—Wolverine's, Deadpool has risen to a level of comic book fame usually reserved for characters decades older than him.

Deadpool shot onto the scene in 1991, his first appearance selling somewhere in the ballpark of 600,000 to 700,000 copies. To put that figure in perspective, even the top comics on the stands today find it a challenge to break the 100,000 mark. While many of those sales could be attributed to the popularity of *The New Mutants*—the title in which Deadpool made his debut—his fame has only grown over the years, outshining even the New Mutants he first battled.

Today, Deadpool has become a permanent fixture in the modern Marvel Universe. Often making guest appearances in other titles, the charismatic hit man with a heart of slightly tarnished gold has even been known to steal the show on variant covers for other characters' comic books in which he's not normally featured. No notable comic convention in the world is complete without a few dozen Deadpool cosplayers, and every mall in the United States has Deadpool T-shirts, knickknacks, and vinyl toys for sale. However, the character's popularity really hit the stratosphere in 2016 with the release of the Deadpool movie—an unlikely R-rated blockbuster that smashed box office records around the world.

The character that started as a minor villain in a comic about an X-Men spin-off team has developed into an entire franchise. While originally created by Rob Liefeld and Fabian Nicieza, Deadpool has now been amended and reinterpreted by countless pencillers and inkers, writers and colorists. This book showcases many of these interpretations, from the earliest depictions of the character to his most recent renditions in both ink and pixels. In order to truly understand Deadpool, you need to witness him at his most serious, most goofy, most kind, and most cruel. But as you're flipping through these pages, keep in mind that to Deadpool, the fourth wall means very little. So while you're looking at him, he might just be looking right back.

PAGE 2 Deadpool sets his gun sights on Agent X. [Cover art by Skottie Young from *Cable & Deadpool* #38, May 2007]

PAGE 4 No form of death or destruction can ruin Deadpool's mood. [Cover art by David Lopez from *X-Men: Battle of the Atom* #1, November 2013]

PAGE 5 Deadpool outfits Spider-Man in classic 1990s comic book armor. [Art by Skottie Young from *The Amazing Spider-Man* #611, January 2010]

OPPOSITE It's "Deadpool: The Musical" when the merc stars in a singing-and-dancing extravaganza. All the dialogue in this special issue was meant to be read to the strain of several famous show tunes. [Cover pencils by Ryan Stegman; inks by Michael Babinski from *Deadpool* (Vol. 2) #49.1, March 2012]

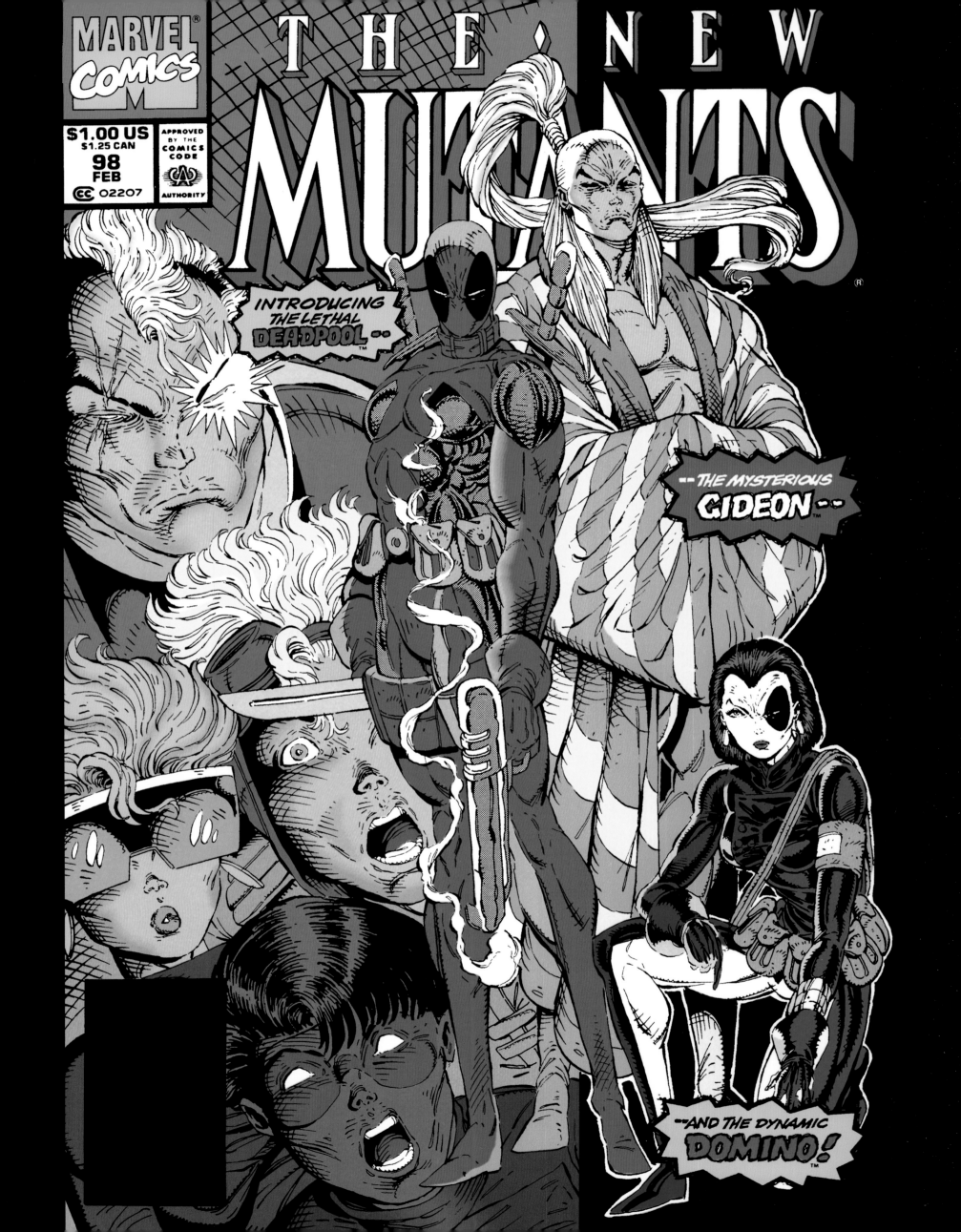

CHAPTER 1
CREATING A NEW MUTANT

In 1991, Marvel ruled the roost when it came to comic book sales. A new generation of superstar artists had burst onto the scene, and comic fandom had taken notice. Todd McFarlane was applying his dynamic pencils to *Spider-Man*, causing the character to virtually leap off the pages. Jim Lee was breathing new life into *The Uncanny X-Men* with a flashy style grounded in exaggerated realism. And Rob Liefeld's stylistic pencils had helped give the X-Men's sister title, *The New Mutants*, a shot in the arm.

Rob Liefeld first met future collaborator Fabian Nicieza, a talented writer with a full-time staff position at Marvel, when Liefeld was still working for DC Comics. Prior to their collaboration, Nicieza had been working his way up the ladder as a writer on titles including *Psi-Force*, *New Warriors*, *Alpha Flight*, and *The Avengers*. "We wanted the chance to work together at some point," says Nicieza. "When the *New Mutants* editor, Bob Harras, decided that he wanted all of Rob's energy and ideas unleashed by plotting the book as well as drawing it, Rob and Bob agreed that I could be a good fit scripting the stories."

At Marvel Comics, Liefeld originally worked with writer Louise Simonson on *The New Mutants*, and the two co-created the adult version of Cable, the grizzled adult son of X-Man Cyclops, who had only appeared as a child in earlier stories. When editor Bob Harras opted to replace Simonson with Nicieza, the change led to the genesis of a comic book legend—Nicieza's first scripted issue of *The New Mutants* would introduce the title's most infamous and memorable villain to date.

Deadpool was an assassin for hire, clad from head to foot in a brilliant red and black suit that hid his identity from opponents. But what was more striking than the expert fighting techniques this villain displayed when taking on Cable and his comrades was his patter—Deadpool had a tongue as sharp as his blades and a wit as deadly as his intentions.

While audiences wouldn't know his history until years later, Deadpool was actually a survivor of the same program responsible for granting Wolverine his unbreakable Adamantium skeleton, a classified operation known only as Weapon X. A mercenary diagnosed with cancer, Deadpool had tried to cheat death by entering this top-secret government program. The result was an extended lifespan granted by the mutant healing factor grafted into his DNA. But in his first appearance in *The New Mutants* #98 (February 1991), this was all still a mystery and, as far as the readers were concerned, Deadpool was merely an unknown killer for hire, one blessed with the gift of gab.

It was Nicieza who gave Deadpool his infamous "mouth," but it was Liefeld who conceived the majority of the character's background. "Deadpool's design and a breakdown of his basic backstory tying him in to Wolverine's continuity were all in Rob's back pocket until he had the chance to showcase the character," says Nicieza. "I took my cues from Rob's descriptions of the character being like 'Spider-Man fighting a tank [Cable]' and from my strong

OPPOSITE Deadpool makes his dramatic debut. [Cover art by Rob Liefeld from *The New Mutants* #98, February 1991]

ABOVE Deadpool shows Cable just how he gets his kicks.
[Pencils by Greg Capullo; inks by Al Milgrom from *X-Force* #15, October 1992]

desire to create a voice that was unlike what you'd expect from a mercenary and unlike the tonal range of the other, more serious, characters in the story. I thought the sarcastic attitude would play well against Cable, and the fans enjoyed their brief, spirited interaction."

Although primarily inspired by Spider-Man and Wolverine, two of Marvel's biggest hits, the Deadpool character also drew inspiration from a third, unexpected source. Liefeld had grown up a fan of DC Comics' *The New Teen Titans* and had based some elements of Deadpool's look on one of that team's main adversaries, the cutthroat mercenary named Deathstroke the Terminator. Even Deadpool's alter ego—Wade Wilson—was a play on Deathstroke's real name, Slade Wilson. But when Deadpool debuted in the pages of *The New Mutants*, it only took a handful of speech bubbles for readers to realize that Deadpool was something entirely new.

Facing Cable, Deadpool made a point of introducing himself and revealing that he'd been hired by the nefarious Mr. Tolliver to not just find the time-traveling warrior but also kill him. Full of bravado and with an incongruously easygoing attitude, Deadpool let Cable know just what kind of mercenary he was, saying: "So when I frost your sorry old mechanical butt, don't take it personally, okay?" After only two pages, Cable figured out exactly what the readers had already deduced: Deadpool was a bizarre, off-the-wall villain with a case of verbal diarrhea. As Cable put it, "You talk too much."

Deadpool's first appearance was short and sweet. While he fought well against the New Mutants, he was soon subdued by a character calling herself Domino, who arrived on the scene at just the right moment to throw a few sharp blades into his back. The mysterious mercenary was soon bound, gagged, and mailed back to Tolliver, sending a clear message that Cable and his allies were not to be messed with.

By this time, *The New Mutants* had generated plenty of buzz and a huge readership. Marvel opted to capitalize on that success by changing the title's name to *X-Force* and starting over with a new first issue. Featuring a team of mutant activists led by Cable, *X-Force* gave new readers a perfect jumping-on point. The title debuted in August 1991, a few short months after *The New Mutants'* 100th and final issue. Billed as a collector's item, *X-Force* #1 came poly-bagged with a free trading card and was later reprinted using gold foil. More important, the title cemented the continuing working relationship between Fabian Nicieza and Rob Liefeld.

Deadpool's return wasn't just a necessary story beat; it was also the result of the overwhelming reception from fans. "One reason Rob and I always laugh when people talk about Deadpool's 'recent popularity' is that within days of *New Mutants* #98 coming out, we received a ton of letters from fans," says Nicieza, "like 600 percent more mail than *New Mutants* usually got—and as an X-book, it always had above-average mail response from fans. Since I worked in

the office, I actually grabbed the stack out of the mail room and personally read each one before they were delivered to the editors, and nearly 75 percent of that mail said, 'This guy was funny, bring him back.'"

The fan mail soon resulted in a lot more exposure for the Merc with a Mouth. "Deadpool was given one of five trading cards to be inserted into *X-Force* #1—which sold like six million copies," says Nicieza. "When he appeared again in *X-Force* #2, we put Deadpool on the cover, and that issue sold almost two million copies. Everyone knew very early on that the character had some juice."

Nicieza and Liefeld worked using the traditional "Marvel Method." Instead of Nicieza writing out a full script and then presenting it to Liefeld to illustrate (as is the common practice today), Liefeld did the initial plotting as he drew. "I waited for Rob's layouts to come in with his plot notes, and then we would talk the issue through before I would script it," says Nicieza. "Schedules were pretty tight, too, so things were a bit hectic, in a crazy but energetic way."

X-Force #2 debuted in September 1991 and featured the first appearance of Garrison Kane (also sometimes called Weapon X) and the first hints at Deadpool's origin. In that issue, Deadpool was hired again by Tolliver, this time to snatch some sensitive Japanese software. While fighting Kane, Deadpool let slip a few personal tidbits, namely that he despised Weapon X and its sister organization, Department H. X-Men fans automatically recognized those familiar government institutions from Wolverine's origin story. This was the first real indication to the readers that Deadpool might share a common background with Marvel's famous feral mutant and might indeed also be a result of the nefarious Weapon X program.

While *X-Force* continued its popularity streak, the increased exposure and fanfare made little difference to Nicieza at the time: "You have to remember, I was writing six or seven titles a month [and the] average sales [for those books] were about 1.5 million comics a month, so even as successful as *X-Force* [was], it wasn't the only thing I was doing that was generating strong sales for the company."

TOP While he put up an impressive showing against the New Mutants, Deadpool is ultimately taken captive by Cable's team. [Art by Rob Liefeld from *The New Mutants* #98, February 1991]

OPPOSITE Rob Liefeld's stylized pages often place emphasis on the characters rather than on the backgrounds and other details. In this example, the technique forces the reader's eye directly to Deadpool's defeat by the Domino imposter. [Art by Rob Liefeld from *The New Mutants* #98, February 1991]

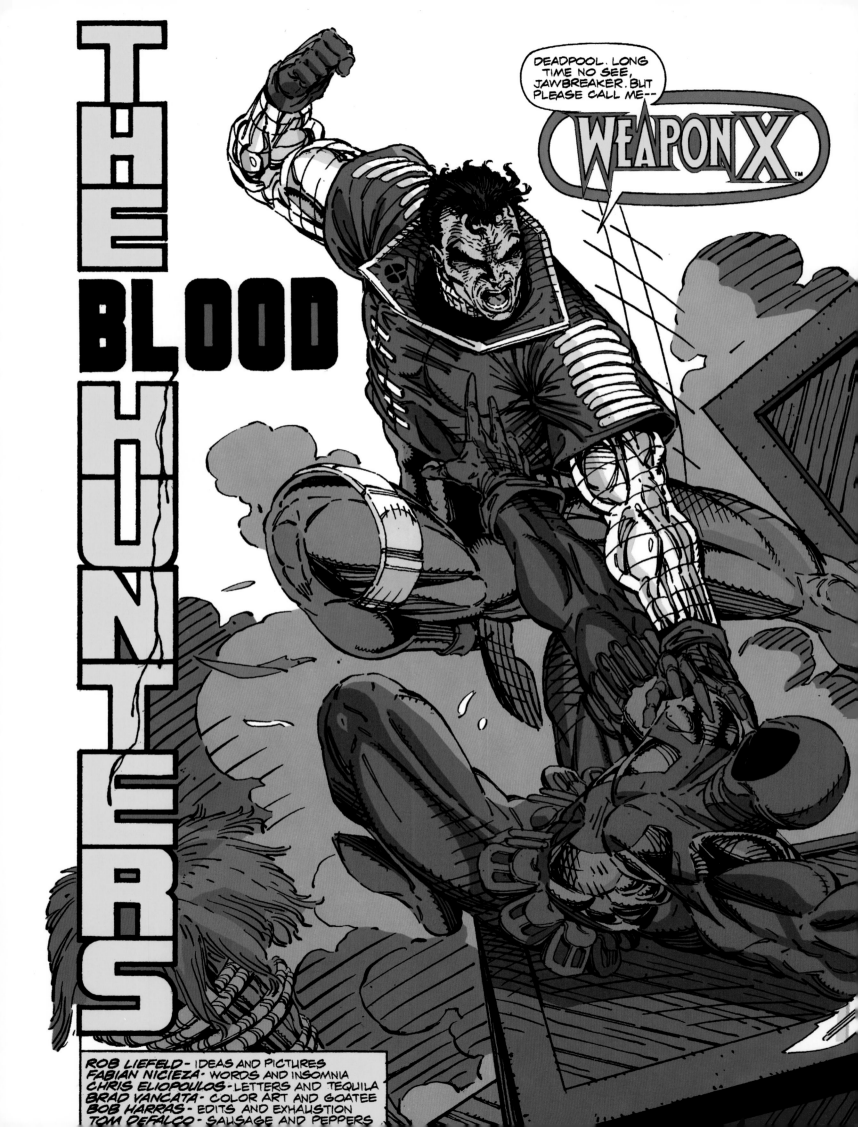

Yet it remained hard to ignore Deadpool's popularity. The mutant continued to pop up in the pages of *X-Force*, running violent errands for his employer, Tolliver. The Merc with a Mouth would not only help retrieve X-Men villains Juggernaut and Black Tom Cassidy in issue #5; he'd also defeat mutant hero Shatterstar in issue #11—once again proving himself to be a highly efficient agent. Issue #11 would also expose more of Deadpool's past, as X-Force member Domino was revealed to be the shape-shifting Copycat, aka Deadpool's former girlfriend, Vanessa Carlysle. Another piece of the complex Deadpool puzzle clicked into place when Copycat revealed that Deadpool's real first name was Wade.

While Deadpool continued to live on at Marvel, Rob Liefeld soon left his creation behind to cofound the company Image Comics with several other leading lights from the industry, including Todd McFarlane. Nicieza stayed on *X-Force*, however, ensuring Deadpool's voice remained consistent even as the artists who depicted him varied. Greg Capullo soon became *X-Force*'s new ongoing artist, helping Nicieza reveal more about Vanessa, Deadpool's healing factor and teleportation skills, and the aftermath of Tolliver's death, as the Merc with a Mouth suddenly found himself without his number-one client. Deadpool was beginning to be sculpted and shaped into a well-rounded character, but it became clear that a team book like *X-Force* wouldn't allow Nicieza the room he needed to thoroughly delve into the mercenary's past. It was time for Deadpool to get a shot at his own title.

OPPOSITE AND ABOVE Garrison Kane has the same code name as the program that forged Wolverine's Adamantium bones: Weapon X. Kane first appeared in this issue, which also marked Deadpool's second appearance. [Art by Rob Liefeld from *X-Force* #2, September 1991]

CHAPTER 2
FROM VILLAIN TO ANTIHERO

In 1993, Deadpool graduated from being a frequent guest star in *X-Force* to appearing in his own four-issue miniseries. As Deadpool's co-creator and the writer who'd handled his appearances to date, Fabian Nicieza was the logical choice to continue to expand on the character's past and present. Artist Joe Madureira lent his lively pencils to the mix, with Mark Farmer and Harry Candelario each inking two issues. The series was subtitled "The Circle Chase" and dealt with the fallout from Tolliver's death. But the real draw for Deadpool fans was in the details.

As Deadpool hunted for Tolliver's will, fans learned the merc's surname was Wilson. It was also confirmed that Deadpool had indeed been in the Weapon X program, and had fought alongside Garrison Kane as well as a man named Gregory Terraerton (who would become the cyber-morphing villain Slayback), during their "good old days." More about Vanessa Carlysle was revealed, including her true blue (skinned) form. And the biggest revelation of all: Deadpool was unmasked, revealing his hideously scarred face for the first time, as readers also learned that, in his past, Wade had been diagnosed with cancer and had gone through chemotherapy treatment at least three times.

It wasn't long before Deadpool would appear in a second miniseries, albeit handled by a different team. Writer Mark Waid made his Marvel debut at the title's helm, invited to write the mercenary as a direct result of his work for the company that Marvel Comics legend Stan Lee often called the "Distinguished Competition." "I was approached by the X-Men editorial office," says Waid. "Apparently, I'd come to their attention through my Flash work for DC Comics."

Although quite familiar with Marvel in general, Waid wasn't as familiar with the character he was tasked with writing: "Honestly, while I knew who Deadpool was, I'd never read any of his stories. Fortunately, at that point, you could count all of [the issues] on the fingers of two hands, so there wasn't a whole lot of research to be done."

A clear choice for the title, Mark Waid had made a splash in the comic book community by combining humor with drama, with entertaining and sometimes powerful results. It seemed that not only was he right for Deadpool, but Deadpool was also right for him. "I much prefer writing comedy, but there just aren't many places for that in—of all things— comic books today," says Waid. "That said, there's always some moment of humor or some element of it in all my work, I think. My influences are pretty eclectic—the movies of Albert Brooks, the great sitcoms of the 1970s like *The Odd Couple* and *The Mary Tyler Moore Show*, and the works of Harvey Kurtzman and Jack Cole, to name but a few. But when it came to Deadpool, I was specifically influenced by Bugs Bunny cartoons. In my mind, Deadpool was Bugs, Juggernaut was a mix of the Tasmanian Devil and Yosemite Sam, and Black Tom was Daffy Duck."

The second Deadpool miniseries was to be more ambitious than its predecessor and include a wider range of mutant characters, their presence helping to boost sales thanks to the exceptional popularity of Marvel's X-Men titles. X-Men regular Banshee and his daughter Siryn played major roles, as did familiar X-Men villains Black Tom Cassidy and his frequent partner Juggernaut. "To tell the truth, that was an editorial edict that came with the assignment," says Waid, "but it wasn't a hardship; I'd always liked Banshee, and I came to really enjoy Deadpool and Siryn's relationship."

OPPOSITE Swordplay on the outside of the issue; wordplay on the inside. [Pencils by Ian Churchill; inks by Bud LaRosa from *Deadpool* (second miniseries) #1, August 1994]

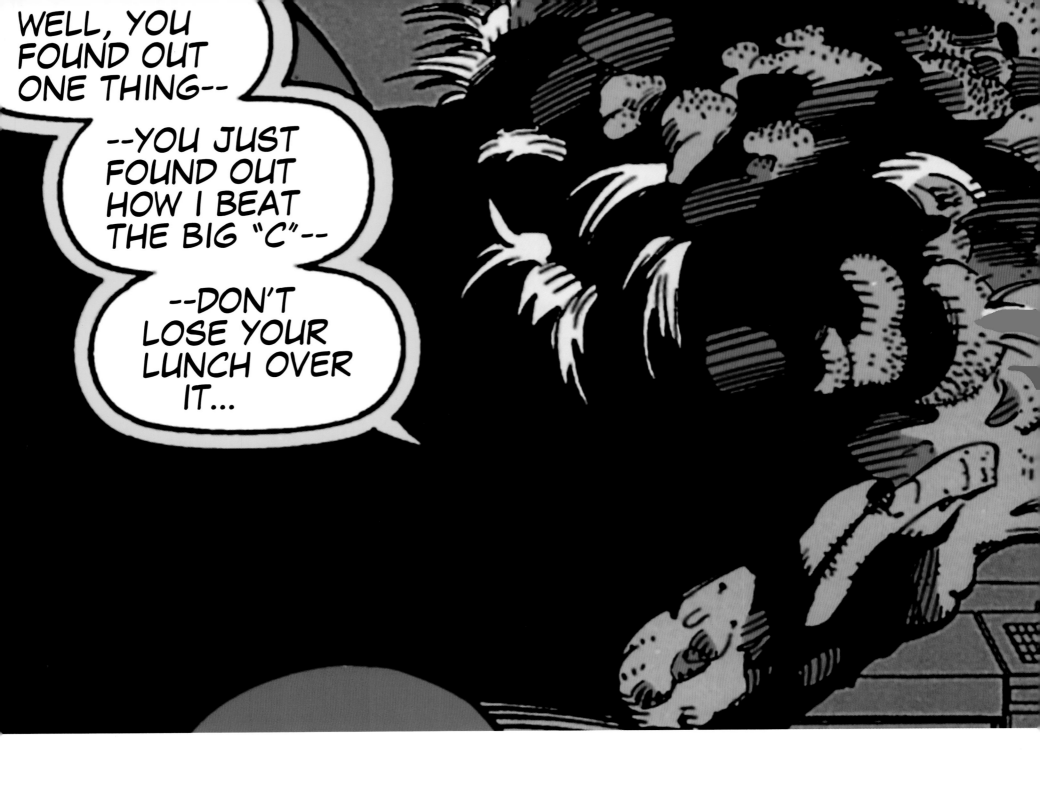

Joining Waid on the title was penciller Ian Churchill and inker Jason Minor. Lee Weeks and Ken Lashley provided additional pencils, and Bob McLeod, Bud LaRosa, and Tom Wegrzyn contributed additional inking as well. Churchill would go on to pencil the fan favorite Superman/Batman and Supergirl titles for DC. "Ian was certainly a joy to work with," says Waid. "As per Marvel's request, I worked plot/dialogue—handing in a detailed panel-by-panel plot, then scripting from the finished artwork." But, in these pre-Internet days, as Ian was located across the pond in England and Waid lived in the United States, the two didn't communicate directly, but through their editor, Suzanne Gaffney.

Waid and Churchill's Deadpool miniseries debuted in August of 1994, one year after the original miniseries hit stands. It introduced a scientist named Killebrew, a self-proclaimed "genetics jockey" who was the lead doctor overseeing the experiments on Deadpool during his time at Weapon X. The plot also revealed a shared history between Banshee and Deadpool, and perhaps most importantly, the series set up a flirtation between Deadpool and Siryn—she would become Deadpool's ongoing love interest for years to come.

Although he didn't put much effort into standard heroics, Deadpool was nevertheless on the verge of becoming a genuine hero. In fact, when Black Tom Cassidy stole Deadpool's hand in an attempt to appropriate Deadpool's healing abilities, the Merc with a Mouth opted to simply defeat Cassidy, rather than take his life. In just a few short years, the deadly assassin had become not just likable, but something of a leading man. Teetering on that precarious line between good and evil would become a Deadpool trademark, and while his world was already a far cry from simple black and white, a gray cloud of ambiguous morality was just about to blow in.

ABOVE Deadpool first rears his ugly head. [Pencils by Joe Madureira; inks by Harry Candelario from *Deadpool* (first miniseries) #3, October 1993]
OPPOSITE BOTTOM LEFT Deadpool's occasional ally Weasel rescues his partner with a devastating show of pyrotechnics. [Pencils by Joe Madureira; inks by Harry Candelario from *Deadpool* (first miniseries) #3, October 1993]

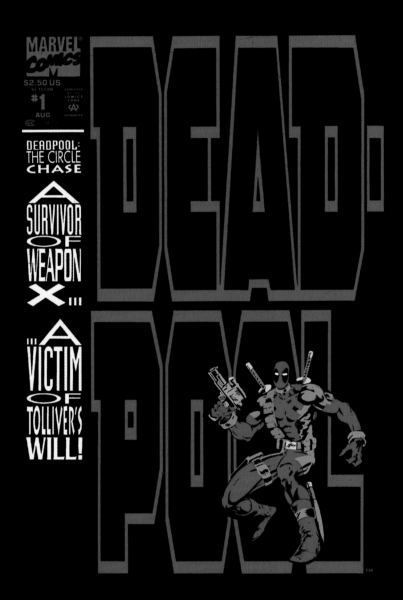

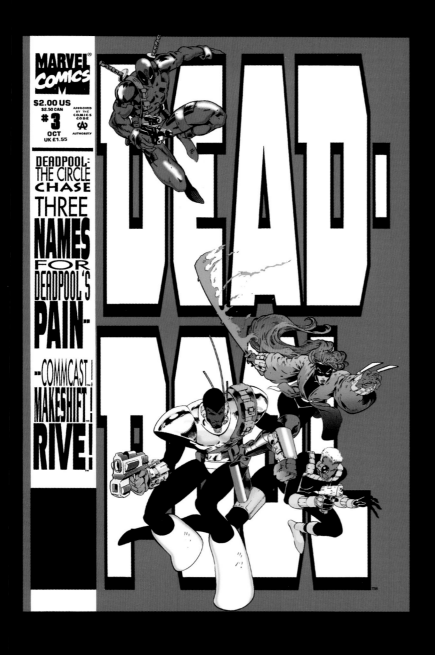

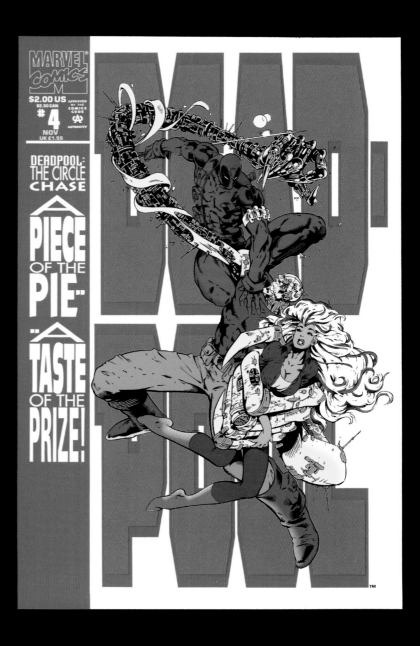

PREVIOUS PAGES The covers for Deadpool's first four-issue miniseries featured a stretched-out version of letterer Todd Klein's Deadpool logo. Klein designed this logo by hand in the days before he worked digitally. [Art by Joe Madureira and Mark Farmer from *Deadpool* (first miniseries) issues #1–4, August–November 1993]

OPPOSITE In his second miniseries, the first time the audience sees Deadpool is on this seventh-page splash. Writer Mark Waid and penciller Ian Churchill never shied away from the ugly reality of mercenary life. [Pencils by Ian Churchill; inks by Jason Minor from *Deadpool* (second miniseries) #1, August 1994]

ABOVE LEFT With a little kindness, Siryn (briefly) coaxes Deadpool to the side of the angels. [Pencils by Ian Churchill; inks by Bud LaRosa, Tom Wegryzn, Philip Moy, and W.C. Carani from *Deadpool* (second miniseries) #4, November 1994]

ABOVE RIGHT Writer Fabian Nicieza fleshes out Copycat's character, albeit in a shade of blue. [Pencils by Joe Madureira; inks by Mark Farmer from *Deadpool* (first miniseries) #2, September 1993]

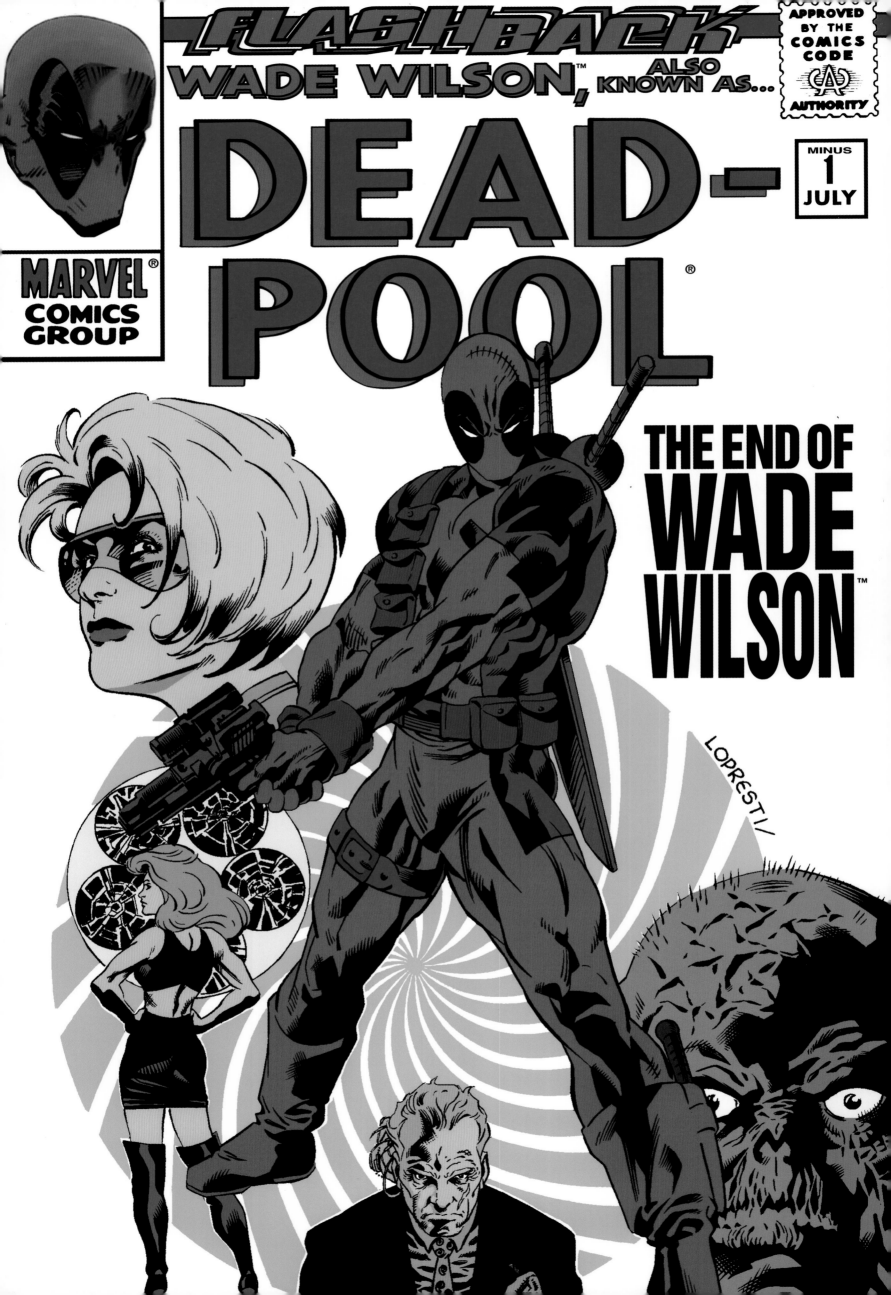

CHAPTER 3
THE MERC WITH A MOUTH

While Fabian Nicieza and Rob Liefeld's impact on Deadpool and his history is undisputed, another writer/artist team—Joe Kelly and Ed McGuinness respectively—are also responsible for making a huge contribution to the character as he's known today.

Kelly and McGuinness were responsible for launching Deadpool's first ongoing series, which debuted with a cover date of January 1997 and ran for over half a decade until its finale, issue #69, published in September 2002. While the title would feature several writers over its lifespan, Joe Kelly would stay with it until issue #33 (October 1999). In that relatively short time, Kelly was able to set the tone for the character, building on Nicieza's work and adding a complex mix of light and dark, superheroics and villainy, reality and science fiction. At this point in his history, Deadpool had appeared in two successful miniseries and seemed to be developing a loyal following, although he was still not quite a proven character like Spider-Man or Wolverine. In addition, the comic book industry itself had also taken a bit of a downturn, causing publishers to be more cautious about which titles they published.

"Matt Idelson was an assistant editor at the time that I started working for Marvel," explains Kelly. "We'd worked together on a few *What If?* books and hit it off pretty well. When the idea of a Deadpool ongoing came along they assigned it to Matt. He asked a few writers to pitch for the book including me, which was a huge honor considering how new I was to the game. That said, he also told me up front that no one expected the book to go past six issues."

Most of Kelly's original pitch never made it to the page, but Idelson liked the direction and voice, and he soon assigned the writer to the title. With comedy influences ranging from Robin Williams to Chuck Jones and Monty Python, Kelly's humor was always an integral part of his work on *Deadpool*. Fortunately for readers, he was partnered with artist Ed McGuinness, who seemed to get the joke. "Ed's a wonderful mad genius," says Kelly. "I was very lucky to meet him at the beginning of his career, and we've been pals ever since. His art has evolved over the years, but it's always carried an energy that was critical to the vibe of *Deadpool*. He's a pleasure to work with, is full of great ideas, and I would say many more wonderful things about him even if he wasn't holding my kids hostage."

With Ed along for the ride, Kelly began concocting his take on Deadpool, working "full script," writing each issue page-by-page, including full dialogue and descriptions for the artist that detailed what was to be depicted in each panel. This method marked a departure from the "plot script" method used in most of Deadpool's past appearances. "Instead of 10,000 monkeys typing at 10,000 typewriters, it's just me in a cage working for bananas and hurling feces for fun," jokes Kelly. "I do work full script, though with the understanding that between the artist and the editor the details are up for grabs so long as the story stays intact. I like to plot out where I'm going on cards or a white board, then I freeze and panic for a while, and somehow in a daze a comic gets written."

OPPOSITE Wade Wilson's origin is examined a bit more in this "minus 1" special. This special was labeled in the negative to imply that it occurred before issue #1 of the ongoing *Deadpool* series. [Art by Aaron Lopresti from *Deadpool* #-1, July 1997]

"In all seriousness," says Kelly, "what I agonize over is the character arc and supporting cast. I want to make sure everyone has a purpose and a journey. Plot isn't as scary, though I can get into trouble if I don't cross my Ts and dot my Is. Then there's the dialogue, which I love. I love jokes; I love dialogue. It's the most fun part of the comic process for me."

It was the creation of a memorable supporting cast that made Deadpool's ongoing series different from the start. The very first issue of the series introduced Hellhouse, a gathering spot for mercenaries that was run by a man named Patch. There, Deadpool would run into regulars like his old friend Weasel and a new villain created for the series called T-Ray. Also introduced in that introductory issue was Deadpool's roommate/prisoner, Blind Al.

Says Kelly, "The main purpose of the supporting cast in any book is to reflect the inner theme and conflicts of the main character. So we stacked the deck against Deadpool as much as possible, surrounding him with terrible people . . . Then there would be one or two friends scraping to keep him in the light. Blind Al's a good example. Because Wade hated his face, he'd only live with a blind person. Because of his past, their relationship was never crystal clear—she was his prisoner but also his verbal sparring partner. She could leave at any time but chose to stay to make up for her own sins. And lastly, because of his ego, he thought he deserved a butler, so we named her after that famous butler from the Distinguished Competition,' Al. She was born specifically to fit into his world." In addition, the rich supporting cast was partially based on people from Kelly's own life. "My wife. My mom. My friends. My enemies. I'll let history sort out who is who."

LEFT The first issue of Deadpool's ongoing series came in the form of a giant-size special with a wraparound cover. [Pencils by Ed McGuinness; inks by Norman Lee from *Deadpool* #1, January 1997]

The first issue of *Deadpool* gave Ed McGuinness and his inkers, Nathan Massengill and Norman Lee, a real chance to shine in an oversized issue that costarred Sasquatch, from the super-hero team Alpha Flight. It also featured the intergalactic firm of Landau, Luckman, and Lake, an institution that, throughout the course of Joe Kelly's run, would become instrumental in making Deadpool the very savior of humanity. By issue #25 (February 1999), LL&L had helped groom Deadpool as their chosen one, pitting him against a powerful entity called Tiamat in a battle from which Deadpool emerged the victor.

The series saw Deadpool operating out of his San Francisco home—dubbed the "Deadhut"—attempting to make a living from various contracts, including fighting government oppressors in the Bolivian jungle and trying to destroy a gamma-radiation facility in Antarctica. It also featured appearances by Siryn, the Hulk, and Daredevil villains Typhoid Mary and Bullseye.

Despite being based in the Golden Gate city, Deadpool headed to the Big Apple for a crossover with Daredevil in a 1997 annual penciled by Bernard Chang and written by Kelly. To this day, Kelly considers it "one of the most gorgeous annuals I ever read, let alone worked on." But there was a reason behind Kelly's fondness for Daredevil and his supporting cast. "I wrote Daredevil for almost a year as I was getting Deadpool off the ground," he says. "Since I was so steeped in Daredevil's world and 'controlled' some of his supporting cast, it was easy for me to cross-pollinate. They also worked extremely well together as opposite ends of a spectrum, so it was great to pit them against one another—and all that red in one book! Awesome."

Ed McGuinness didn't stay on the ongoing Deadpool title past issue #9, and while his presence was missed, Joe Kelly and editor Matt Idelson found several talented replacements, including Pete Woods, a relative newcomer who would go on to contribute to a variety of high-profile DC Comics titles including *Robin* and *Action Comics*. While the series and the character continued to develop, Kelly enjoyed the freedom of working on a character that had yet to register on Marvel's radar as an A-list solo star. "In the beginning, as I said, no one expected us to break six issues so they were definitely not paying attention to what we were doing, which was awesome," says Kelly. "Matt, Ed, and I were in our own little bubble, making each other laugh. Pete joined the party as well and we had a ball. *Deadpool* #11 was a direct result of Matt's 'let's try anything' spirit as an editor. It was a glorious time."

In that memorable comic, dubbed internally as the "Forrest Gump" issue, Deadpool and Blind Al traveled back into Spider-Man's past, as Deadpool impersonated Peter Parker, and Blind Al did her best impression of Parker's elderly aunt, May. It was Kelly and Woods' way of inserting Deadpool into the fabled Marvel Age of Comics in the

-- UNFORTUNATELY, IT'S *ALSO* THE WAY OF THE JUNGLE TO CALL IN *REINFORCE-MENTS.*

THUSLY, THE *PREY-TURNED-PREDATOR* AGAIN BECOMES *PREY* --

-- PRAYING THAT THE PREDATORS IN *PURSUIT* ARE AS *POOR* WITH *PROJECTILES* AS THEIR PRESENTLY *PULVERIZED PALS.*

WHAT I WOULDN'T GIVE TO BE MARLIN PERKINS RIGHT ABOUT NOW...

HEY, IT'S DEADPOOL!

Stan Lee Presents:

or... DEADPOOL #1

Joe Kelly
Story
Ed McGuinness
Pencils

Nathan Massengill
with Norman Lee
Inks

RS/Comicraft/DL
Letters

Chris Lichtner
Colors
Digital Chameleon
Enhancement
Matt Idelson   Harras
Editor   Chief

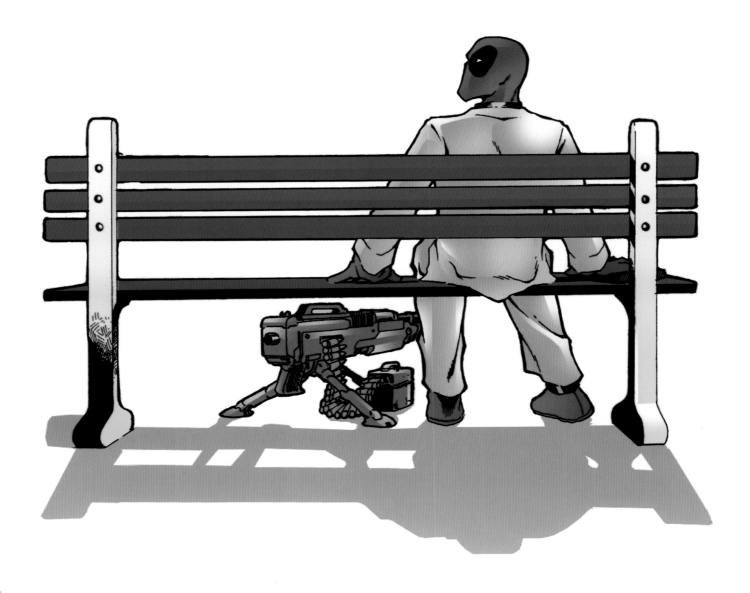

STAN LEE PRESENTS A VERY SPECIAL DEADPOOL BROUGHT TO YOU ACROSS THE VAST EXPANSE OF SPACE AND TIME BY:

JOE "MARTY MCFLY" KELLY WRITER • PETE "H.G. WELLS" WOODS PENCILER • NATHAN "TIME TRAVELLER™" MASSENGILL INKER ("90s)

AL "TIME BY SEIKO" MILGROM AND JOE "SPACE WARP" SINNOTT INKERS ("60s) • CHRIS "SAGAN" SOTOMAYOR COLORIST

R "TIMECOP" S AND COMICRAFT/EMERSON MIRANDA LETTERING • PAUL "TIME WARP AGAIN" TUTRONE ASSISTANT EDITOR

MATT "TIME TO MAKE THE DONUTS" IDELSON EDITOR • BOB HARRAS TIME LOOP • BOB HARRAS TIME LOOP • BOB HARRAS TIME LOOP • BOB HARRAS TIME LOOP • BOB HARRAS TIME LOOP

BASED IN PART on AMAZING SPIDER-MAN #47 by STAN LEE and JOHN ROMITA, Sr.

SPECIAL THANKS TO DARREN AUCK, THE BULLPEN (AND ALL THAT NAME ENCOMPASSES) PATTI DAZZO, RALPH MACCHIO, KAREEM MONTES, WILSON RAMOS, REPRO, POND SCUM

AND OF COURSE STAN AND JOHN FOR ALLOWING THIS TRAVESTY TO OCCUR!

With Great Power comes Great Coincidence

1960s, just as Forrest Gump was inserted into key events in American history in the popular film. The issue also featured a few of Marvel's less shining stars, including a super-hero team that never quite got off the ground. Says Kelly, "Pete Woods was responsible for a groundbreaking issue and made the Great Lakes Avengers cool—that's a feat!" The issue even earned Spider-Man co-creator Stan Lee's seal of approval. "I melted," Kelly says of his reaction upon hearing that Lee liked his issue.

Perhaps what made Joe Kelly's take on Deadpool so memorable was that he didn't shy away from the cruel realities of a killer for hire. The writer even went so far as to reveal how unstable Deadpool truly was by having the Merc with a Mouth shut Blind Al in "The Box"—a bizarre torture chamber of sorts—thereby reminding readers that Deadpool was not a character to idolize. "It always felt right to me that Deadpool was an antihero in the truest sense of the word," says Kelly. "The guy came from an awful past, was a merc who had done terrible things—ignoring all of that just to make him into a super hero would have been false. We went through great pains to force Wade to attempt to reconcile his past with his desired future, usually to much pain and degradation.

"It's also important to note that my brain is wired for 'dark.' I love uncomfortable psychological stuff, and applying that to the genre of super heroes is a sweet spot for me. Add in death's-head humor and I'm home. So remember, I am not well in the head. I think that the fans were on board. In general I've always felt that we struck the right balance between light and dark in a fun and unexpected way."

As Kelly's run neared its close, the writer opted to unleash his most controversial story yet. It involved the mysterious figure from Deadpool's past called T-Ray. "T-Ray started out as a cool-looking badass who became a villain thanks to something Deadpool had done in the past," says Kelly. "They both knew it, and T-Ray would never ever buy into the 'I'm trying to be a hero' routine. Then as time went on it struck us that there's no real reason to believe that Deadpool was always 'Wade Wilson,' so what if he'd stolen that identity from T-Ray back when he was a more despicable human being?"

The twist was revealed in issue #33 of the series. Deadpool had been a low-level merc called "Jack," who had been taken in by a kindly couple with the last name Wilson. The story ended with the Wilsons presumed dead and Deadpool stealing the identity of Wade Wilson for himself. Meanwhile, the real Wade Wilson survived the encounter and returned to plague Deadpool as T-Ray. "It was a very dark story," says Kelly, "one that I think we would have stretched a lot of pathos out of if we had been able to do the whole thing . . . it was a great way to flip a hero and his major villain on their head."

That issue was Kelly's last, putting a dramatic ending on a series full of cliffhangers. "Once we got into the third year of the book, the cancellation threats began," says Kelly. "We kept dipping below the publishing threshold; I'd be told to wrap things up, but then fans would rally and write letters, and we'd get a stay of execution. This happened three separate times in my memory, and each time I had to interrupt a story just to restart it again. I loved that the fans were saving us, but after a while I couldn't take the ups and downs anymore, so I sadly left the book."

But Deadpool's first ongoing series didn't end there. Says Kelly, "Clearly, it didn't get canceled . . . my crystal ball is cracked." Following Joe Kelly's departure, Christopher Priest became the book's newest scribe, originally teamed with pencillers Paco Diaz and Gus Vasquez, and inkers Rod Ramos and John Holdredge. Priest and company would take Deadpool into uncharted waters, removing his supporting cast for the most part in favor of setting the Merc with a Mouth up with new roommates, the super villains Constrictor and Titania. During Priest's run, which featured the artwork of penciller Jim Calafiore among other artists, Deadpool would join the Frightful Four (a villainous group that's often seen as the antithesis of the Fantastic Four), see his face magically healed for a short period of time thanks to Loki, and even battle the Avengers and Black Panther.

After Priest left the title following issue #45, writer Jimmy Palmiotti and artists Paul Chadwick and Ron Randall pitted Deadpool against the world of organized crime when the Merc with a Mouth was hired to kill New York City's top six mob bosses. Palmiotti was later joined by cowriter Buddy Scalera as he continued his run. As a variety of artists came and went on the title, Copycat re-entered Deadpool's life, as did his short-lived partner Kid Deadpool.

When writer Frank Tieri came on board starting with issue #57, things went from bad to worse for Deadpool. With pencillers Georges Jeanty and Jim Calafiore illustrating his ongoing misfortune, Deadpool was recruited into the renewed Weapon X program against his will, forcing him to team up with demented murderers like Sabretooth and starting a chain of events that left Deadpool literally dead and buried. With his life apparently at an end, Deadpool thought he could finally retire into the arms of his waiting love, Death—the physical manifestation of the ultimate end in the Marvel Universe and the woman he had been infatuated with for years. However, just as Deadpool was about to embrace Death's icy touch, T-Ray returned to bring him back to life. T-Ray was acting in the employ of Thanos, another of Death's suitors and a powerful cosmic villain who had sworn to never allow Deadpool to rest in peace.

As a result, not even Death herself could keep Deadpool on the sidelines of the Marvel Universe, or at least that's how it seemed. In reality, the editors at Marvel had a new plan up their sleeves, and in a few short months, there would no longer be a Deadpool comic book at all.

OPPOSITE Deadpool gets the last laugh even in death. The title for Deadpool's death storyline, "Funeral for a Freak," is a direct parody of the famous "Death of Superman" chapter from DC Comics entitled "Funeral for a Friend." [Art by Alvin Lee of UDON from *Deadpool* #63, April 2002]

FOLLOWING PAGES Marvel bleeds red as Daredevil and Deadpool find themselves uneasy allies. [Cover pencils by Bernard Chang; inks by Jon Holdredge from *Daredevil/Deadpool* '97 Annual, July 1997]

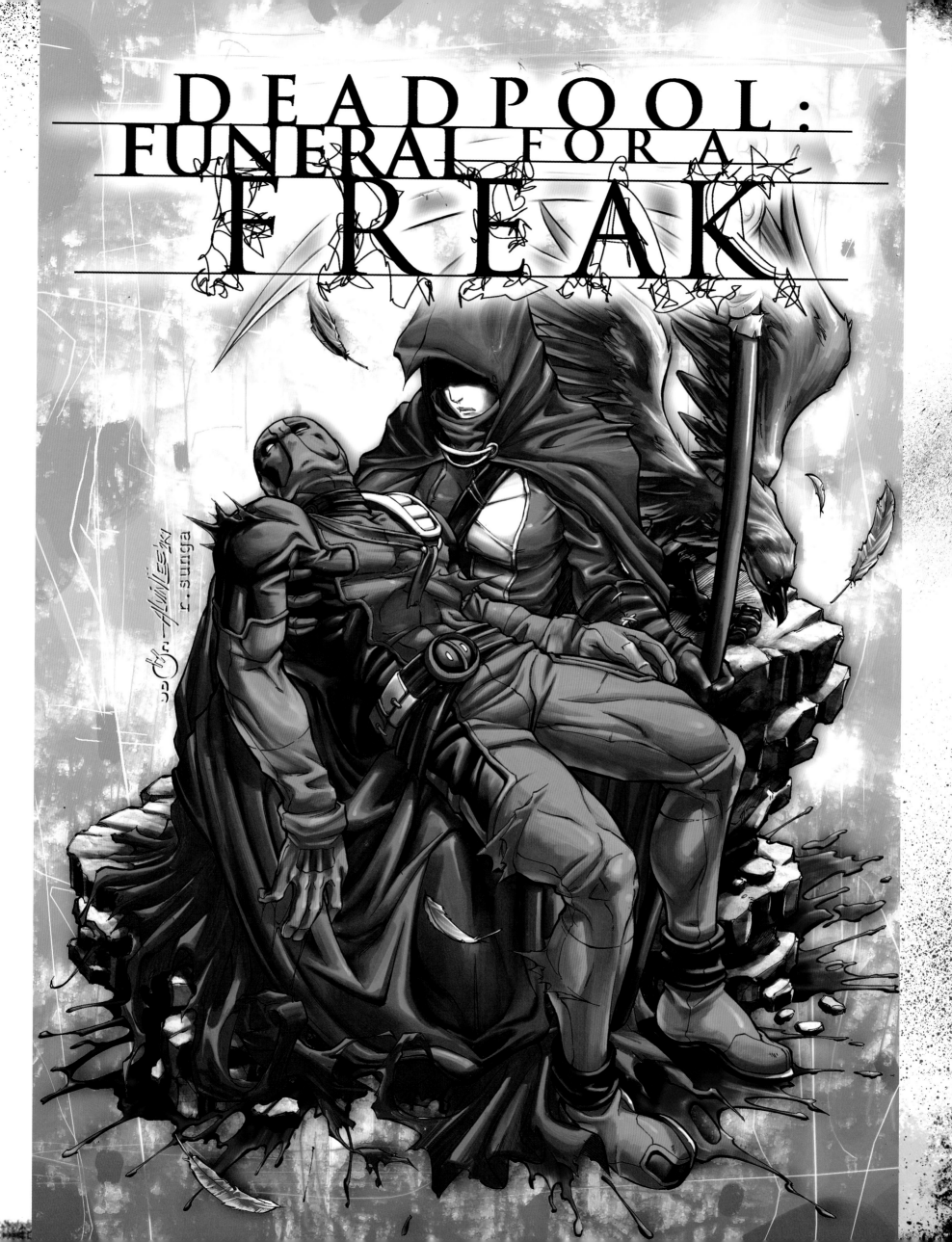

OPPOSITE *Deadpool* #11 featured the character's first parody cover: a homage to the iconic cover of Spider-Man's first appearance in 1962's *Amazing Fantasy* #15. [Pencils by Pete Woods; inks by Nathan Massengill from *Deadpool* #11, December 1997]

ABOVE LEFT Peter Parker's longtime love interest, Mary Jane Watson, makes her highly anticipated debut. Writer Stan Lee had teased her first appearance for months, finally revealing her face in this memorable panel. [Art by John Romita from *The Amazing Spider-Man* #42, November 1966]

ABOVE RIGHT Writer Joe Kelly and penciller Ed McGuinness parody Mary Jane Watson's first appearance. In their version, Deadpool is introduced to a woman more his speed—the nefarious Daredevil villain Typhoid Mary. [Pencils by Ed McGuinness; inks by Norman Lee and Nathan Massengill from *Deadpool* #6, June 1997]

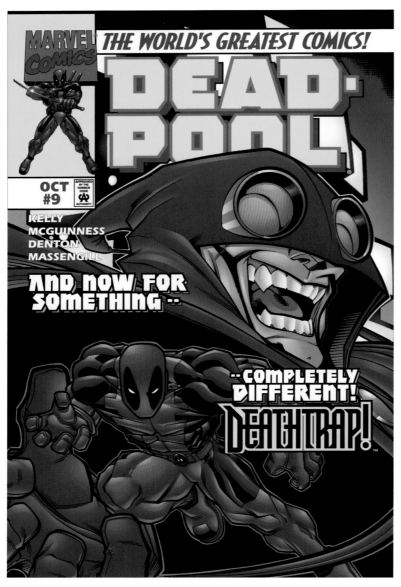

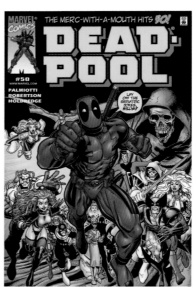

ABOVE LEFT Deadpool meets one of his very own super villains in the form of Deathtrap. [Pencils by Ed McGuinness; inks by Nathan Massengill from *Deadpool* #9, October 1997]

ABOVE TOP RIGHT The Monkey with a Mouth. [Art by Dan Norton from *Deadpool* #36, January 2000]

ABOVE BOTTOM RIGHT Known for his detail work, artist Arthur Adams handles Deadpool and his supporting cast in a fiftieth-issue extravaganza. [Art by Arthur Adams from *Deadpool* #50, March 2001]

OPPOSITE TOP LEFT Clashing with the Hulk is one way to drive up sales on a fledgling comic book. Who knew the Merc with a Mouth would also be adept at marketing? [Pencils by Ed McGuinness; inks by Nathan Massengill from *Deadpool* #4, April 1997]

OPPOSITE TOP RIGHT Unlike G.I. Joe, Deadpool is nobody's hero, American or otherwise. [Pencils by Jim Calafiore; inks by Mark McKenna from *Deadpool* #42, July 2000]

OPPOSITE BOTTOM LEFT Deadpool doesn't take extraterrestrial threats too seriously on this cover that parodies the *Alien* movie poster. [Art by Cully Hamner from *Deadpool* #40, May 2000]

OPPOSITE BOTTOM RIGHT Famous for the shadowy and realistic style he often employs on *Punisher* covers, artist Tim Bradstreet lends his craft to Deadpool as the Merc with a Mouth faces off against the notorious Frank Castle. [Art by Tim Bradstreet from *Deadpool* #55, August 2001]

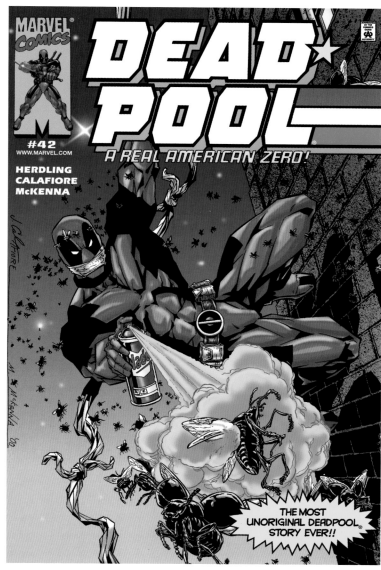

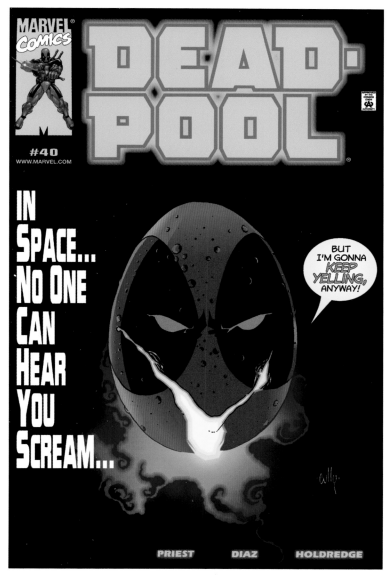

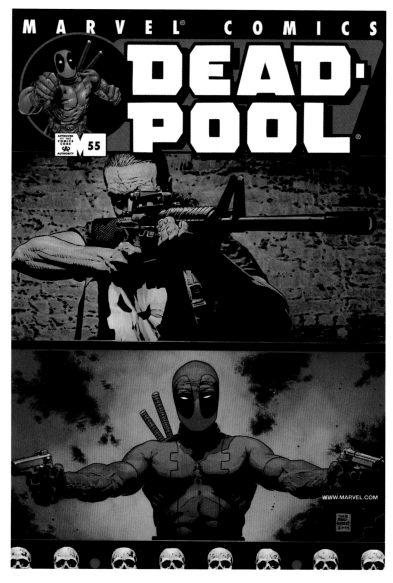

ABOVE Deadpool proves a bit too impatient for the drawing process in this bonus pinup page. [Pencils by Rick Leonardi; inks by Jon Holdredge from *Deadpool* #50, March 2001]

OPPOSITE A parody of the iconic *Detective Comics* #38 (April 1940) cover that introduced the world to Batman's youthful partner Robin. This issue showcases Kid Deadpool (who actually debuted in the issue prior). [Art by Darick Robertson from *Deadpool* #51, April 2001]

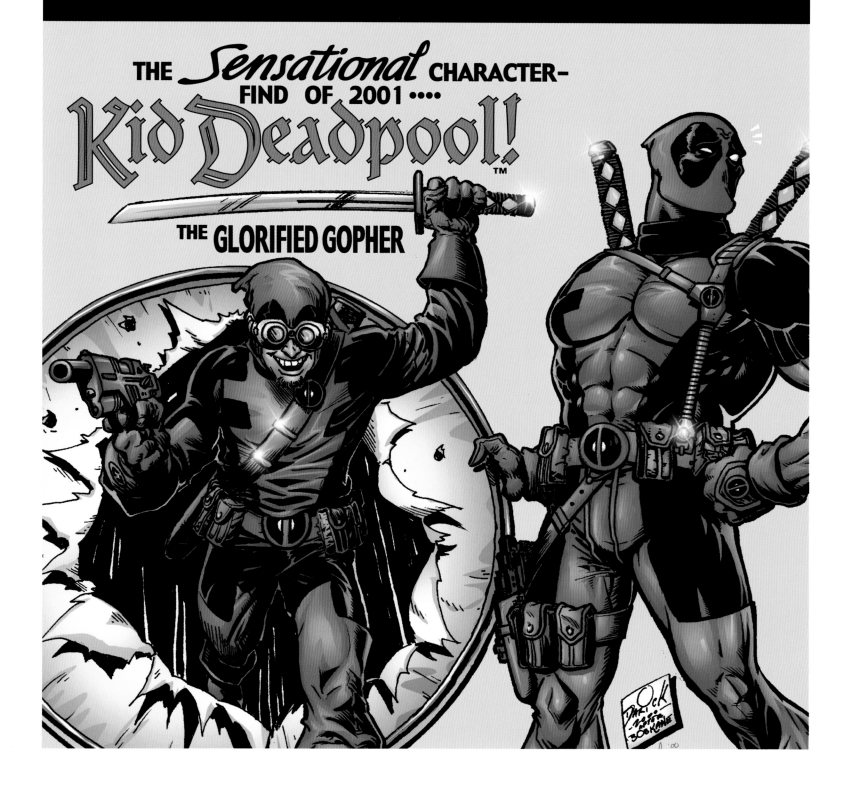

MARVEL® COMICS
DEADPOOL®:
FUNERAL FOR A
FREAK
MARVEL PG
2
62
TIERI
JEANTY
HOLDREDGE

OPPOSITE Deadpool once again finds the opportunity to mock the Distinguished Competition with this cover that pokes fun at the cover of *Superman* (Vol. 2) #75 (January 1993), the issue that saw the death of the Man of Steel. [Art by Georges Jeanty from *Deadpool* #62, March 2002]

ABOVE As Deadpool grew older, his world grew more complicated. This one-shot special serves as a handy text recap of the first few years of the mercenary's comic book life. [Design by Comicraft, Inc. from *Encyclopaedia Deadpoolica*, December 1998]

THE ORIGIN

Joe Kelly was instrumental in giving Deadpool something he'd never had before: a true origin issue. In Deadpool's 1998 annual costarring Death herself, Kelly collaborated with penciller Steve Harris and inker Reggie Jones to reveal that Weapon X, the clandestine organization responsible for coating Wolverine's bones in Adamantium, was just the tip of the iceberg when it came to the creation of Deadpool's abilities. Unlike Wolverine and other survivors of the Weapon X program, Deadpool was not a mutant before he underwent the organization's unorthodox medical procedures. Kelly revealed that the Merc with a Mouth's time at Weapon X had little effect on him and only served to scar his body for life. He was placed in a hospice, and expected to die. There, he and the other residents participated in a "deadpool" of sorts, betting on who would next meet Death. Experimented on by Dr. Killebrew and his assistant Ajax, Deadpool was finally pushed to the brink, suffering mental and physical torment that successfully activated the healing factor grafted to his DNA. "Steve Harris drew Deadpool's heartbreaking origin story with class and finesse," says Kelly.

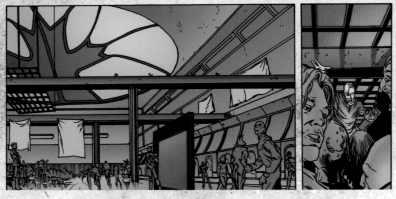

OPPOSITE AND ABOVE Wade Wilson arrives at Dr. Killebrew's hospice and is soon transformed into the gruesome- looking Deadpool fans know and love. [Art by Steve Harris and Reggie Jones from *Deadpool/Death '98 Annual*, July 1998]

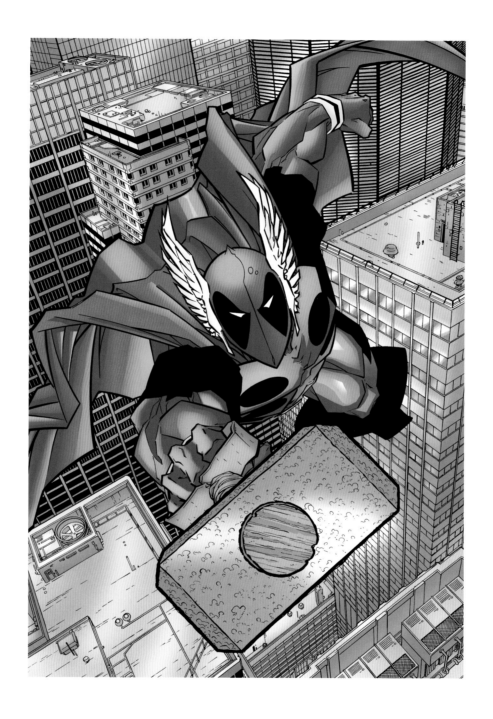

OPPOSITE Deadpool remembers a horror from his past in this two-page sequence written by Joe Kelly. [Pencils by Pete Woods; inks by Rebecca Shelander from *Deadpool* #30, July 1999]

ABOVE Deadpool seemingly wields the hammer of Thor thanks to the trickery of Loki. The fact that his hammer proved to be a forgery didn't dissuade Deadpool from delivering his finest Thor impression, complete with a generous sprinkling of "eths" at the end of random words, including "thinketh," "holdeth," and "understandeth." [Pencils by Jim Calafiore; inks by Mark McKenna from *Deadpool* #37, February 2000]

CHAPTER 4
AGENT X

Deadpool's first ongoing series was about to come to its natural end, but in no way was Marvel ready to close the door on their infamous hit man. It was determined that a change was necessary for both Cable and Deadpool in order to boost sales for the characters and further increase their popularity. Writer Gail Simone was brought on to *Deadpool* with issue #65. Known for her dark humor that could veer from wickedly cruel to downright silly, Simone was a perfect fit to pilot Deadpool's often-unhinged brain and fill out his supporting cast with her usual style and flair. She was partnered with artist Alvin Lee as well as other members of his art collective, UDON Studios, giving the title a completely new look. And right away, the creative team tossed Deadpool into the deep end where he had to sink or swim.

In Simone's story, Deadpool bungled a job in Japan but still seemed to shoot and kill four major crime lords, gaining a massive reputation boost in the process. He soon became the envy of his peers at Merc Works, a gym for mercenaries, and the head of his own mercenary hire company, Deadpool Inc., which he ran with considerable help from his personal assistant, Sandi Brandenberg. He also accepted a new hire, the homeless and mentally unstable Ratbag. However, Deadpool's exploits soon earned him the attention of the Black Swan, a well-to-do assassin who lived in Germany. Soon the readers learned that Black Swan was actually the person responsible for Deadpool's Japan hit. As a result, Black Swan was infuriated that the Merc with a Mouth was taking credit for what was meant to be the Black Swan's final, bloody opus. The story climaxed in issue #69 when an explosion seemed to end the life of both Deadpool and the Black Swan.

Simone's run was highly influential, especially a storyline where Deadpool uses Pym Particles—the innovation that allows Ant-Man to shrink to a minuscule size—on the hulking Spider-Man super villain Rhino, later adopting the miniature Rhino as his pet and even keeping the infuriated villain on his keychain. Says future Deadpool artist Reilly Brown, "There was this storyline where Deadpool shrank the Rhino down to the size of a keychain, and I thought that was hilarious and followed the book regularly after that. Fabian [Nicieza] and I took that same idea and shrank Deadpool himself down for a few issues, which was a ton of fun."

Issue #69 proved to be the last issue of Deadpool's original series. However, shortly afterward, *Agent X*, created by the same team of Gail Simone and UDON Studios, made its debut. In that series, a man with a similar sense of humor to Deadpool and a prominent X-shaped scar on his face showed up at Sandi Brandenberg's apartment, near death. It transpired that this mystery man was a mercenary with a similar healing factor and skill set to that of Deadpool. This turn of events led many readers to theorize that Agent X might be an amnesiac Deadpool simply adopting a new name. Similarly, Cable had also been rebranded with a drastically updated look in a new title called *Soldier X*, lending even more credence to the theory that Deadpool had also undergone a major Marvel makeover.

OPPOSITE The mystery of the man calling himself Agent X begins with the cover of issue #1. [Art by Alvin Lee and Rob Ross of UDON from *Agent X* #1, September 2002]

While the character seemed to have Deadpool's sense of humor and charm, *Agent X* wasn't quite what the readers were expecting, and Simone ended up leaving the title after issue #7. "I think *Agent X* was a delightful series because Gail Simone really can't do wrong," says Fabian Nicieza, "but it was unfairly burdened with being 'not-Deadpool' and that—along with Cable being turned into Soldier X—was more a mistake on the publisher's part than it was by the individual creators working on those books."

After a few guest issues by other writers and artists, Simone was convinced by Marvel to finish off the *Agent X* series, teaming up with UDON Studios once again from issue #13 to the series' conclusion in issue #15. Embracing the supporting cast they had fleshed out in their relatively short tenure, including Sandi, the sharp-shooting mutant Outlaw, and the super villain Taskmaster, Simone and UDON revealed that Agent X was not Deadpool at all. When Black Swan pushed his telepathic powers to the limit during the explosion that seemingly killed Deadpool, the result was a psychic feedback of sorts that imparted Deadpool's personality and healing factor onto a corpse, reanimating it into the man who would be known as Agent X. In truth, both Wade Wilson and Black Swan survived the encounter, and when Black Swan reemerged, both Agent X and Deadpool teamed up to bring down the super villain, even though the two mercenaries seemed to harbor a true hatred for one another.

Although Deadpool had endured a tumultuous time waiting on the sidelines, Marvel wasn't quite ready to give him another go at a solo title. Instead, they opted to revitalize Cable and Deadpool's respective titles in a truly unique way: by combining them.

ABOVE LEFT AND ABOVE RIGHT Deadpool and Agent X share a lot of similarities, as these two covers penciled by Alvin Lee serve to demonstrate. [Art by Alvin Lee and Arnold Tsang of UDON from *Agent X* #14 and #15, December 2003]

OPPOSITE TOP LEFT Agent X features artwork heavily inspired by Japanese comics, as this faux supply catalog cover clearly shows. [Cover by Ken Siu-Chong of UDON from *Agent X* #5, January 2003]

OPPOSITE TOP RIGHT Evan Dorkin serves as guest writer on this first installment of a two-part Agent X tale that features a guest art team as well. [Cover pencils by Juan Bobillo; inks by Marcelo Sosa from *Agent X* #10, May 2003]

OPPOSITE BOTTOM LEFT Artist Brian Stelfreeze helps put the "X" in Agent X on this dynamic cover. [Art by Brian Stelfreeze from *Agent X* #12, August 2003]

OPPOSITE BOTTOM RIGHT Agent X acquired quite the supporting cast, despite his comic book's relatively short tenure. [Cover art by UDON from *Agent X* #13, November 2003]

OPPOSITE Deadpool's not a fan of cheap shots—unless he's making them. [Art by Alvin Lee, Rob Ross, Eric Vedder, A-Zero, and TR2 of UDON from *Deadpool* #65, May 2002]

ABOVE LEFT AND ABOVE RIGHT Deadpool finds an enemy in the form of Spider-Man rogue Rhino and an ally in the Avengers' villain Taskmaster. When it comes to a personality so polarizing, it's often hard to predict how established characters will react to Deadpool's particular brand of antics. [Cover art by Angelo Tsang of UDON from *Deadpool* #66; Cover art by Alvin Lee and Rob Ross from *Deadpool* #68, June and August 2002]

ABOVE Deadpool's creative use of Pym Particles to ward off the charging Rhino is the stuff of comic book legend. [Art by Alvin Lee, Rob Ross, Eric Vedder, A-Zero, and LTRZ of UDON from *Deadpool* #66, June and July 2002]

OPPOSITE Many people mistook Agent X for Deadpool during the early days of X's career, including Rhino. The villain wanted payback for the humiliation he suffered as the Merc with a Mouth's "pet." [Art by Alvin Lee, Eric Vedder, Rob Ross, Calvin Lo, Shane Law, TheRealTI, and Omar Dogan of UDON from *Agent X* #6, February 2003]

OPPOSITE When Agent X first emerges on the scene, he resembles Deadpool in both his scarred visage and his cartoon-like personality to the point that even Deadpool's personal assistant, Sandi Brandenberg, is confused. [Art by Arnold Tsang, Andrew Hou, Eric Vedder, Omar Dogan, and TheRealT1 of UDON from *Agent X* #1, September 2002]

ABOVE Outlaw, another former ally of Deadpool, joins Agent X's crew, sensing something familiar about the mysterious mercenary. [Cover art by Alvin Lee and Rob Ross of UDON from *Agent X* #2, October 2002]

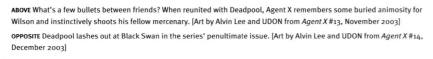
ABOVE What's a few bullets between friends? When reunited with Deadpool, Agent X remembers some buried animosity for Wilson and instinctively shoots his fellow mercenary. [Art by Alvin Lee and UDON from *Agent X* #13, November 2003]

OPPOSITE Deadpool lashes out at Black Swan in the series' penultimate issue. [Art by Alvin Lee and UDON from *Agent X* #14, December 2003]

CHAPTER 5
THE ODD COUPLE

*I*n 2004, both Cable and Deadpool seemed to need a facelift. The two heroes had been revamped (and in Deadpool's case, replaced) to varying degrees of success, and it was time to bring back the familiar characteristics that made readers like them in the first place. And who better to spearhead a return to form than the writer responsible for much of their original characterization—Fabian Nicieza.

Says Nicieza, "I actually hadn't worked for Marvel for several months when editor Mike Marts called and said, 'We've been talking about the problems we've been having with Cable and Deadpool and your name came up as someone who knows both characters. You think a book with the two of them together could work?' And I said, 'Of course, it would be great!' And then when I got off the phone, I thought, 'Crap, how the hell am I ever going to make a book with these two work?'"

While Cable and Deadpool debuted in the same era of the early 1990s and had come to blows from time to time, the characters had little in common, aside from a mutual history with X-Force. The invention of the title *Cable & Deadpool* was the perfect excuse to team up this odd couple in classic "buddy cop" fashion, letting Deadpool's oddball personality play off of Cable's serious demeanor. The only question that remained was how Nicieza was going to get them together in the first place.

The series began with Deadpool sitting alone in front of his television set, a man devoid of purpose and a social life when not out chasing down the target of a mercenary contract. "From panel one of page one of issue one where we open with Wade all alone, binge-watching TV, waiting for a life, [it] was all pure me writing the character the way I saw him," says Nicieza.

Obviously back at home with his creation, Nicieza invented the idea of the One World Church, an organization of religious zealots who hired Deadpool to steal a virus from a German facility. It was there that Deadpool came into conflict with Cable, and the story progressed until the two were infected with the prototype biotoxin, which forced them to literally merge together after being reduced to liquid form. They separated when Cable used his telekinesis to return to solidity. He then literally vomited out the liquid Deadpool, the merc reforming when outside Cable's body. While the two were back to the land of the living, this melding thoroughly interfered with Cable's famous "bodysliding" teleportation ability. From that point on, every time Cable activated a bodyslide, Deadpool teleported with him, the two linked in a bizarre fashion that allowed Nicieza to have a lot of fun with their already fractious relationship.

Handling the art of the first two issues was penciller Mark Brooks, one of the talents who'd go on to influence another of Nicieza's future Deadpool collaborators, artist Reilly Brown. After Brooks, Patrick Zircher took over the penciling chores on the title with issue #3. "Patrick really was my partner on the title during our run together," says

OPPOSITE Cable and Deadpool kick off their series with guns blazing. [Cover art by Rob Liefeld from *Cable & Deadpool* #1, May 2004]

Nicieza, "and we'd established a strong working relationship having done *Thunderbolts* for two years together. He is immensely talented and an excellent storyteller who brought a lot of great ideas and visual bits to the title. I didn't find a steady collaborator on the book that I could share that kind of communication with until Reilly Brown came aboard."

Zircher stayed on the title for nearly two years, with Rob Ross and UDON Studios handling the inks, before finishing his run with issue #24. During that run, he and Nicieza brought back Deadpool and Cable's familiar look and feel, but the duo also expanded the characters' horizons. Readers watched as Cable set himself up as a messiah of sorts, forming a utopia called Providence Island that was seemingly the template for his own perfect society. Meanwhile, Cable was stuck with Deadpool as an unlikely partner and was forced to send him on missions to keep him busy, including an assignment that forced Deadpool into conflict with the villain Black Box. Through all the chaos, it was the clash of personalities at the heart of the book that really allowed Nicieza's comedic writing to shine.

"I tend to draw the humor in Deadpool based on the character reacting to a situation rather than creating a situation for the character to react to," says Nicieza, who cites an eclectic mix of comedic influences from *The Mary Tyler Moore Show* to *M*A*S*H*. "In that regard, I don't think of myself as a 'comedy writer,' because I think they create comedic situations to plug their character into, or develop stories based on the comedic situations they want to see their character react to. Because I've never really written a monthly Deadpool book, when writing *Cable & Deadpool*, I tended to develop the plot and then generate Deadpool's reactions as a result [of] what was happening in the story rather than have the story react to him."

64

OPPOSITE Fabian Nicieza instantly sets the scene in *Cable & Deadpool* #1 by crafting a memorable moment- to-moment sequence that succinctly establishes just how meaningless Wade Wilson's life would be without his Deadpool alter ego. [Art by Mark Brooks and Shane Law of UDON from *Cable & Deadpool* #1, May 2004]

BOTTOM RIGHT One of Nicieza's favorite scenes: Deadpool's attempt at filling out Marvel Girl's costume. [Pencils by Patrick Zircher; inks by Rob Ross and M3th of UDON from *Cable & Deadpool* #9, January 2005]

Those early issues of *Cable & Deadpool* also saw Nicieza's favorite scripted Deadpool moment, when the Merc with a Mouth attempted to blend in with the X-Men in issue #9 by dressing as Marvel Girl and insisting, "Once an X-Man, always an X-Man!" Of course, the X-Men weren't too keen on the idea, with Beast reminding Deadpool that not only was he not an X-Man, he wasn't even a mutant.

While Nicieza seemed to slip back into the role of Deadpool's wordsmith rather easily, his style of writing had changed significantly since his original collaborations with co-creator Rob Liefeld. "I worked 'Marvel method' for half of my career, which was plot first and once the pages were drawn, then do the script," says Nicieza. "The industry norm changed about fifteen years ago and most editors preferred full scripts, so that's how I worked on *Cable & Deadpool* and most titles since 2004. I still prefer plot first, but I understand why some writers and artists might not."

Guest artists Lan Medina and Staz Johnson filled in here and there, but *Cable & Deadpool* soon fell into the capable hands of artists Ron Lim and Reilly Brown, who would alternate story arcs or issues to take the title to its conclusion at issue #50. "Ron is the first artist I worked with on a monthly book when we did *Psi-Force* for Marvel's New Universe and he is just the nicest, most positive guy in the world," says Nicieza, "The word 'professional' has his face by it in the dictionary. We hadn't worked together for a long time when he did some *Cable & Deadpool* issues, and pairing up with him was like riding a bike."

Nicieza's other collaborator, Reilly Brown, was fairly new to comics, and especially Deadpool. "Well, Reilly now is different than Reilly when we first worked together," says Nicieza. "He was younger and *Cable & Deadpool* was his first regular book, so the rookie working with the whiny arrogant veteran isn't a great combination. That being said, I recognized Reilly's skills immediately, and not just his storytelling or drawing skills, but his understanding of character and his sense of humor, both broad and subtle. Reilly just kept improving as we worked together, so by the time our run was over, he was ready to rock and roll on any assignment he got."

"*Cable & Deadpool* was my first major project at Marvel, and it was a ton of fun to work with the writer who first came up with Deadpool," says Reilly Brown of Nicieza. "I was a fan of the character before I ever drew him, though. I first started reading his adventures regularly in 2002."

Brown was thrown into the deep end on *Cable & Deadpool*, a title that required excellent visual storytelling to convey its serious and dramatic beats. To first learn how to tackle the title characters, Brown looked to his artistic influences. "For Deadpool, I'm probably mostly influenced by Alvin Lee, who was drawing him when I first started

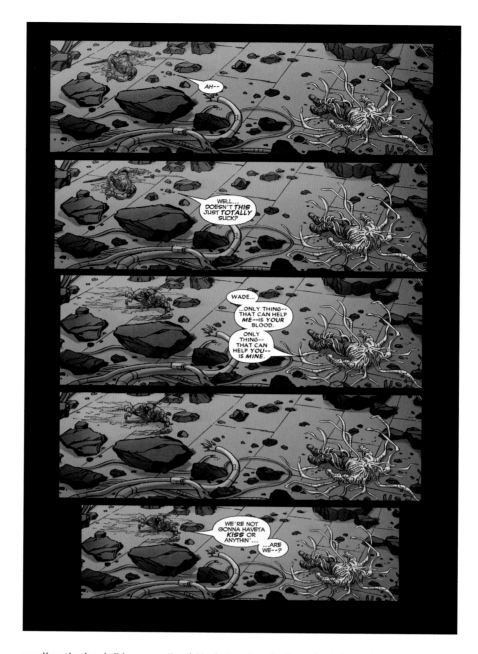

reading the book," he says, "and Mark Brooks who launched the *Cable & Deadpool* series that I started on. When I was first figuring out how to draw the character, those are the issues I was referencing the most."

"When I started *Cable & Deadpool*, I hadn't read any of the previous run of the title," says Nicieza. "I hadn't read Joe Kelly or Christopher Priest or Gail Simone's runs. And I didn't want to unless or until I was going to use aspects of the continuity they'd established." As *Cable & Deadpool* continued, Nicieza would do just that, bringing in aspects from Deadpool's original series, and even *Agent X*. One of the first times he referenced existing plot points was through a rematch between Rhino and Deadpool, with Deadpool losing the fight this time around and becoming a human keychain. Soon after, Nicieza and Brown brought back Agent X, as well as his sidekicks Sandi and Outlaw. In the process, however, they decided to make Agent X morbidly obese, shot by an experimental Hydra weapon that altered his physical form. This was also the storyline that introduced one of Nicieza and Brown's most famous creations: Bob, Agent of Hydra. A silly sidekick/pet that Deadpool has kept over the years, Bob even found his way into the Deadpool feature film in a cameo role.

"Seeing Bob in the movie was a real trip!" says Brown. "I wasn't expecting that at all. His appearance was perfect! Just a totally generic henchman whose life we get to learn a bit more about, and then he gets punched in the face. Exactly how a Bob appearance should go! Bob is such a fun character . . . it's something I've always thought about for all the goons and henchmen who appear in action stories; those are all people who have lives outside of working for the super villain of the month, but we never get to learn much about who they are, or why are they helping to take over the world. In Bob's case, it turns out, [he's working for a super villain because he needs] health insurance."

As Bob joined the cast and Deadpool began to operate Agency X, employing Sandi, Outlaw, and Agent X, another familiar face from Wade Wilson's past reemerged: his longtime arch-nemesis, T-Ray. In a story for *Cable & Deadpool* #39, penciled by Ron Lim and inked by Jeremy Freeman, Deadpool essentially proved T-Ray's memories

OPPOSITE When dealing with an unpredictable threat like Deadpool, Cable prefers to take no chances. Instead, he opts to literally blow the mercenary's mind, a tactic that proves effective on more than one occasion. [Art by Mark Brooks and Shane Law with Chris Stevens from *Cable & Deadpool* #2, June 2004]

ABOVE By the end of this issue, things aren't looking too hot for the title characters. [Pencils by Patrick Zircher; inks by Rob Ross and Alan Tam of UDON from *Cable & Deadpool* #4, August 2004]

67

incorrect, seemingly contradicting the past storyline by writer Joe Kelly in which Deadpool stole the Wade Wilson name. Just like the original story it was referencing, this new T-Ray tale caused some controversy among Deadpool fans. "There were some fans who were pissed, there were some who didn't care," says Nicieza. "That tends to be the norm when you muck around with earlier stories. I try not to 'erase' other people's stories too often, because when it's been done to me, I don't enjoy it. By the same token, I thought a lot of the aspects of the T-Ray story just didn't work, made the character's backstory way more convoluted than it needed to be, and generated far more problems than it solved. All that being said, I tried very hard to do it in such a way that as a reader, when reading a character like Deadpool, you can believe whatever you want to believe, and if it's not 'true' now, chances are it will be true in two weeks."

Marvel opted to end *Cable & Deadpool* with its fiftieth issue, and as the title neared its conclusion, the character of Cable was killed off as tensions on Providence reached a head. Although Cable's death would prove temporary, this freed up the title to allow Deadpool to team up with other Marvel Universe stalwarts, including Wolverine, Captain America, and the Fantastic Four. It also allowed Reilly Brown to stretch his creative muscles, even trying his hand at writing. "My first experience plotting a story was back in *Cable & Deadpool*, when Fabian had to leave the book two issues before it ended," says Brown. "There was a bunch of ideas that we'd talked about that I wanted to make sure I got the chance to draw, so I didn't want another writer swooping in and mucking it all up, so I wrote my own story and pitched it. You always know when an artist is writing the story because there will be aliens and dinosaurs fighting! Or in my case, Venomosauruses—dinosaurs with alien symbiotes. Luckily Fabian was able to come in and round out the dialogue in the end, so that the series had a consistent feel, and the characters had a consistent voice throughout. I'm really happy with how that series ended."

Nicieza agrees. *Cable & Deadpool* reached fifty issues in April of 2008, drawing one of his favorite series to a close. "As far as issues I'm proud of," says Nicieza. "I have to be honest and I think the entire run was pretty damn good . . . and some of my strongest, most consistent work."

OPPOSITE After saving each other's lives through a bizarre melding process, Cable and Deadpool initially don't realize how interconnected their lives have become. [Pencils by Patrick Zircher; inks by Rob Ross and UDON's M3th from *Cable & Deadpool* #5, September 2004]

ABOVE Deadpool and Agent X meet once again, mirror images of one another, brimming with hatred. [Pencils by Patrick Zircher; inks by UDON's M3th with Derek Fridolfs from *Cable & Deadpool* #12, April 2005]

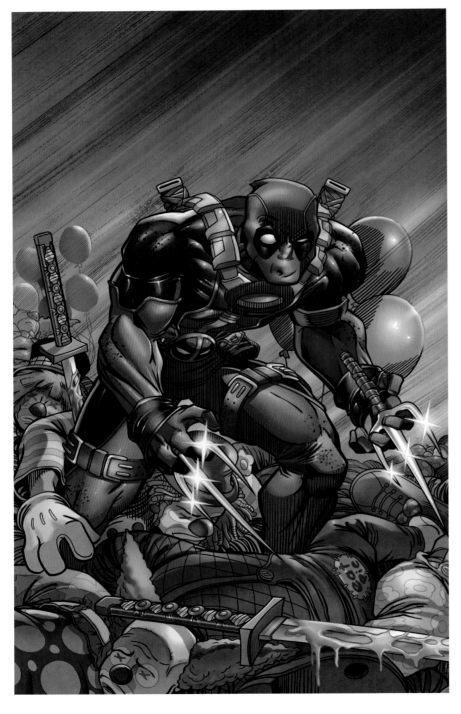

ABOVE LEFT AND ABOVE RIGHT Deadpool's tradition of inspired parodies continues, shamelessly lifting the composition from John Romita Jr.'s classic cover for the first chapter of the Wolverine saga "Enemy of the State." [Pencils by Patrick Zircher; inks by M3th of UDON from *Cable & Deadpool* #15, July 2005]

OPPOSITE Never the best of friends, Spider-Man and Deadpool have seemingly even less in common than Cable and Deadpool. [Cover pencils by Patrick Zircher; inks by M3th of UDON from *Cable & Deadpool* #24, March 2006]

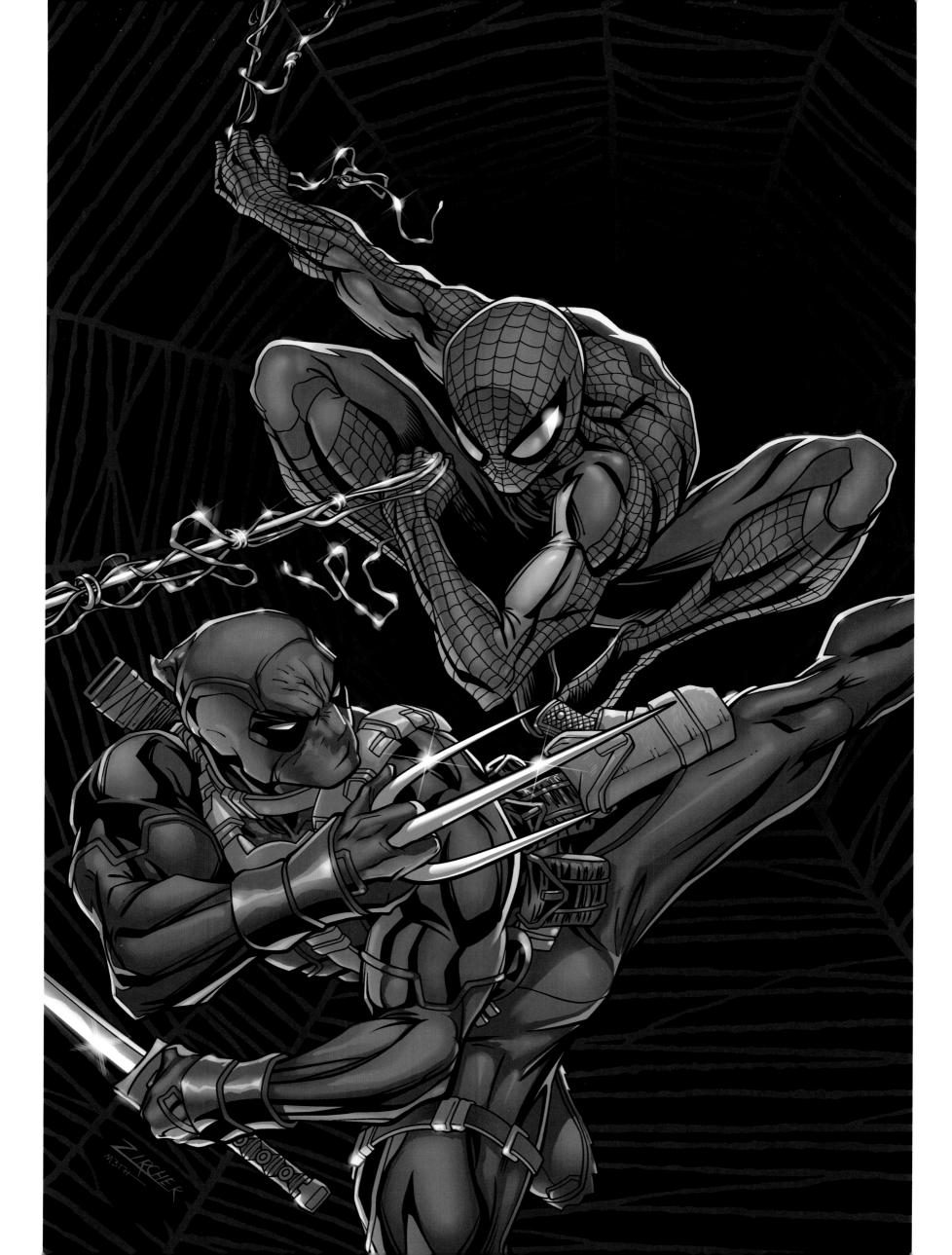

OPPOSITE It's Deadpool: Private Eye when there's a murder on Cable's island home of Providence. [Cover art by Patrick Zircher and M3th of UDON from *Cable & Deadpool* #13, May 2005]

TOP LEFT AND TOP RIGHT Rob Liefeld returned to two of his favorite co-creations when he rendered the covers of the first four issues of *Cable & Deadpool*. [Art by Rob Liefeld from *Cable & Deadpool* #2 and #3, June and July 2004]

BOTTOM LEFT AND BOTTOM RIGHT Patrick Zircher soon found himself handling the art duties on *Cable & Deadpool's* interiors as well as a series of the covers. [Art by Patrick Zircher and Shane Law from *Cable & Deadpool* #8 and #9, December 2004 and January 2005]

THE BROWN METHOD

Reilly Brown's years on *Cable & Deadpool* helped the artist hone his craft, a process he now has down to a science. "I usually sketch things out digitally on my tablet on the train ride to the studio," says Brown. "I'm drawing really small and really roughly at this point, mainly just trying to get ideas out. When I settle on an idea, working on the tablet makes it easy to make things the right size and put them in the right place. Then I print the rough sketch out at full size and use my light box to transfer it to the final paper. I do it that way because it's good to be able to start the drawing with a clean board, without eraser marks or the shadows of sketches that weren't quite right. I draw it in pencil and then finish it in ink and scan it in to send to the colorist."

But no artist in the comic book industry works alone. Pencillers are often aided by inkers and colorists, as a grueling monthly deadline is always looming. "It's great to be able to ink myself when I can," says Brown, "but because of deadlines I usually have to find someone else to help me out. Jay Leisten and Jeremy Freeman did really great jobs on the *Deadpool & Cable* stuff, and Nelson DeCastro and Terry Pallot were great on *The Gauntlet*. It's always good to know a good inker who can save my ass, and make the art look even better than when I do it all on my own!"

"For coloring, I've lately been working with Jim Charalampidis a lot, who's an amazing talent and keeps getting better," adds Brown. "He knows how to use bright colors that really pop and how to use them to enhance the mood of the scene."

THESE PAGES Reilly Brown got a chance to both plot and draw *Cable & Deadpool* near the end of the title's run. The result is a wacky combination of some of his favorite visual elements: super heroes, villainous symbiotes, and dinosaurs. [Pencils by Reilly Brown; inks by Jeremy Freeman and Bob Almond from *Cable & Deadpool* #50, April 2008]

ABOVE While Wolverine and Deadpool have similar backgrounds, more often than not the two find themselves on opposite sides of any given skirmish. [Pencils by Ron Lim; inks by Jeremy Freeman and John Dell from *Cable & Deadpool* #44, October 2007]

OPPOSITE Deadpool's relationship with Bob, Agent of Hydra, gets off to a rocky start. In this issue, Deadpool manages to make short work of his future sidekick, despite being shrunken in stature following the Rhino's revenge. [Pencils by Reilly Brown; inks by Jeremy Freeman and Pat Davidson from *Cable & Deadpool* #38, May 2007]

OPPOSITE AND ABOVE As Deadpool explores life without Cable, cover artist Skottie Young lends his considerable talents to the title's ever-changing roster of team-up partners. [Art by Skottie Young from *Cable & Deadpool* #44–48, October 2007– February 2008]

CHAPTER 6
THE TITLE CHARACTER

Deadpool's momentum was increasing. Not only had *Cable & Deadpool* renewed interest in the misadventures of Wade Wilson and friends, but Deadpool had begun to steal the show in that title's final issues, proving he was ready to once again go solo. In order to increase sales and serve as a jumping-on point for new readers, a few short months after *Cable & Deadpool* came to a close, Deadpool's second ongoing series hit stands, dated November 2008. Right from the start, Deadpool was thrown into the middle of one of the biggest battles the Marvel Universe had ever seen.

The heroes of the modern Marvel Universe were locked in combat with the shape-shifting alien race known as the Skrulls during the blockbuster miniseries *Secret Invasion*, an event that would lead to immediate repercussions in Deadpool's new book. In fact, in the first issue of the series, Deadpool seemed to give in to his darker side by offering his services to the Skrulls, who quickly rejected him, opting to build an army of their own alien Deadpools from his DNA. Later, Deadpool convinced the would-be conquerors to allow him to train these new clones and ultimately forged an army of duplicates as crazy and unpredictable as he was. The result was a massive defeat for the Skrulls, one Deadpool had planned the entire time, as a secret freelance agent for the heroic government agency S.H.I.E.L.D.

Writer Daniel Way was the creative force behind Deadpool's devious plan, and while he was new to the ongoing series, he was no stranger to the character. Having already penned a rather humorous showdown between Deadpool and Wolverine for *Wolverine: Origins*, Way was familiar with survivors of the Weapon X program, and already had Deadpool's voice down pat. Interestingly enough, Way opted to add a new approach to writing Deadpool's famous inner monologues, adding another set of caption boxes that would often challenge Deadpool's standard yellow thought captions as well as his external dialogue. Now Deadpool had yellow and white captions, constantly at odds with one another despite originating from the same twisted mind. Using this method, Way could let Deadpool argue with his own thoughts, effortlessly showcasing just how mentally unhinged the Merc with a Mouth really was.

With plenty of ideas for Deadpool, Daniel Way was in it for the long haul, writing the second ongoing series all the way to issue #63 (December 2012), the longest consistent run for a writer on the character since its inception. However, the artists on the title would change several times within this series, each leaving a mark or two on Deadpool's look. The first to try his hand was Paco Medina, often with the able Juan Vlasco supplying inks. Carlo Barberi filled in as a penciller from time to time, with Sandu Florea assisting Vlasco on the ink chores here and there as well. Barberi would later become a regular artist on the title (often inked by Walden Wong), eventually drawing more issues than anyone else for this particular series.

In the books, Deadpool hopped from one madcap adventure to the next, battling everyone from Skrulls to corrupt plastic surgeons; he also appeared in a crossover with the super villains of the Thunderbolts and opted for a short career as a pirate. Familiar faces like Bob, Agent of Hydra, once again had their lives thrown into chaos by Deadpool.

OPPOSITE If you're going to save the universe, might as well do it in the pages of a brand-new ongoing series. [Cover art by Clayton Crain from *Deadpool* (Vol. 2) #1, November 2008]

Even Bullseye—now calling himself Hawkeye after having usurped the mantle of that hero—showed up for a rematch with his longtime frenemy. Deadpool also continued his love affair with Death, and was almost united with her permanently when he attempted to join the X-Men, nearly pushing Wolverine past the breaking point.

While familiar faces remained a constant in his second series, new threats also debuted, some more hilarious than others. Perhaps the most famous of Daniel Way's innovations was Hit-Monkey, a hit-man monkey who had no love for Deadpool, but seemed to respect guest star Spider-Man. Deadpool also found the time to get "space-married" after meeting the alien Orksa and seemingly killing her husband, Macho Gomez. While Macho had actually survived the encounter, his "murder" set off a chain of events that culminated in a kiss between Orksa and Deadpool. According to her alien customs, this kiss meant the two were wed. But unfortunately, the cosmic relationship was not to be, and the couple soon got "space-divorced" after Deadpool tangled with Id, the Selfish Moon.

But there was no new threat as deadly as the twisted mirror image of Wade Wilson, appropriately named Evil Deadpool. Grown from a variety of Deadpool's severed body parts collected by obsessive Deadpool stalker and prison employee Dr. Ella Whitby, Evil Deadpool proved just how dangerous the merc could be if he had even less of a conscience.

With help from other artists including Salva Espin, Shawn Crystal, and the teams of Bong Dazo and Jose Pimentel, and Alé Garza and Sean Parsons, Deadpool's second series contained all the trademark visual flair to which readers had grown accustomed. But when Daniel Way moved on to other projects, Deadpool moved on as well, and the second ongoing series came to an end with issue #63 (December 2012). However, there was certainly a light at the end of Deadpool's train-filled tunnel as Marvel once again opted to restart Deadpool's ongoing series in order to spotlight a new creative team. This third volume would begin a month later, in January of 2013.

ABOVE Deadpool doesn't seem to have a type when it comes to romance, as his space marriage proves. [Pencils by Carlo Barberi; inks by Walden Wong from *Deadpool* (Vol. 2) #33, April 2011]

OPPOSITE The well-dressed Hit-Monkey's first meeting with Spider-Man and Deadpool proves explosive. [Cover art by Jason Pearson from *Deadpool* (Vol. 2) #20, April 2010]

Humor had always been an important part of Wade Wilson's sharp-tongued dialogue, and when Marvel renewed his ongoing title to generate more reader interest and spotlight the shift in creative teams, they found a perfect comedy duo to spearhead it. Writers Gerry Duggan, of TV's *Attack of the Show!*, and Brian Posehn, best known as a comedic character actor, took up the task of putting words in Deadpool's mouth. Artist Tony Moore, known for his work on the smash Image Comics success, *The Walking Dead*, would render the first six issues of the series.

The title began with perhaps Deadpool's most off-the-wall caper yet when a necromancer named Michael let loose the ghosts of a horde of former United States presidents. Agent Emily Preston of S.H.I.E.L.D. tasked Deadpool with dealing with the political poltergeists, as she didn't want the public to witness the Avengers battling historical figures. Deadpool managed to subdue them after a few rough battles with the likes of Abraham Lincoln and George Washington, but at a price. Michael unleashed his magic on Agent Preston and Deadpool, which led to Preston's soul being locked in Deadpool's body. Now Deadpool really did have a voice in his head, the voice of his newest supporting cast member.

Deadpool's supporting cast grew sizably during Duggan and Posehn's run. Not only was Preston a major part of Deadpool life—remaining so even after her soul was later successfully transferred into an LMD (Life Model Decoy) robot—but Michael the necromancer also stuck around, joining Deadpool on many adventures. Another supernatural presence, the ghost of Benjamin Franklin, a friendly specter that helped Deadpool battle the ex-presidents, also became a regular. Real-life actor Scott Adsit, of *30 Rock* fame, was introduced into the Marvel Universe in the form of a comic book character that shared his name and likeness (Adsit is a close friend of Duggan and Posehn and a comic book fan, hence the tribute). Adsit was established as an agent of S.H.I.E.L.D. alongside Preston, and stuck around for the majority of the title as well.

Another high point of this third *Deadpool* volume were the flashbacks, set in time periods varying from the 1970s to the 1990s and meticulously rendered by artist Scott Koblish to match various eras in the history of comics. Koblish used the drawing styles prevalent during each decade as an in-joke for diehard comic book fans. And while these tales might be viewed at first as fun one-shot diversions from the main storyline, Duggan and Posehn soon began

OPPOSITE The "Marvel NOW!" initiative saw the relaunch of a variety of titles with the aim of whetting the appetites of fans searching for new titles to collect. [Art by Geof Darrow and Peter Doherty from *Deadpool* (Vol. 3) #1, January 2013]

ABOVE Deadpool does his best Spider-Man impression. [Art by Mike Hawthorne from *Deadpool* (Vol. 3) #10, July 2013]

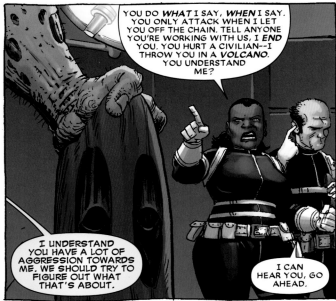

to reveal major plot points in these issues, introducing a character named Carmelita Camacho as a love interest for Deadpool during a cartoonish 1970s flashback where Deadpool became Deadpimp, complete with Afro and gold medallion. While readers didn't know it at the time, the writers had big plans for Carmelita, plans they would reveal in a powerful five-part story called "The Good, the Bad, and the Ugly."

Having lulled the audience into accepting Wade Wilson's silly yet violent world, Duggan and Posehn used this new plot to show readers that the title wasn't going to be all fun and games. In the story, Deadpool learned more about his past, discovering that even after he had been manipulated by the Weapons Plus program (the government initiative that included Weapon X under its umbrella) and treated like a lab rat at Killebrew's hospice, he had spent years in and out of captivity, at the hands of a shadowy individual called Butler. Butler continued Weapon Plus's work, often erasing Deadpool's mind, so that Wilson could not even trust his own memories. Not only that, but he soon learned that Butler had been taking organs from him on an ongoing basis for use in his experiments. Butler finally opted to once again capture Deadpool, also holding Carmelita and her daughter Eleanor hostage. The tension was ratcheted up further when Wade discovered that he was a father: Eleanor was the Merc with a Mouth's daughter.

This powerful series, drawn by Declan Shalvey, saw Deadpool team up with Wolverine and Captain America to shut down Butler's current operations in North Korea, where he had been using Wade's DNA to forcibly imbue helpless test subjects with mutant powers. The result was a modern-day concentration camp housing a slew of horrific "mutates." While Deadpool and his team managed to stop Butler, ending his campaign and his life, Deadpool discovered Carmelita's body among the dead, with no trace of his daughter anywhere.

As Deadpool's third ongoing series continued and he began fighting the organization known as U.L.T.I.M.A.T.U.M., Wade was also busy simultaneously starring in an additional title by Duggan and Posehn—one in a strikingly different format than his standard monthly comic book. The series was called *Deadpool: The Gauntlet*, and was an "Infinite Comic"—a series originally created for the Internet, featuring comic panels that progressed as the reader clicked through the story. These panels allowed characters to seemingly move through the scene, creating an illusion of

ABOVE Actor Scott Adsit made the jump from sitcoms to funny books as a S.H.I.E.L.D. agent. [Art by Tony Moore from *Deadpool* (Vol. 3) #1, January 2013]

OPPOSITE If Deadpool were a low-budget 1970s exploitation film, it might look a little like this cover. [Art by Kris Anka from *Deadpool* (Vol. 3) #13, September 2013]

motion that could be compared to watching a digital flipbook. Supplying the art for this thirteen-part series that began in January 2014 was an artist familiar to Deadpool fans, Reilly Brown. "Those guys are a lot of fun," says Brown about his storytelling partners, Duggan and Posehn. "I was mainly in contact with Gerry, and we'd talk on the phone about once a week, shooting ideas back and forth. Gerry loves his '80s pop culture references!"

"With the Infinite Comics, the artist inevitably has to take a larger role in plotting how the story plays out, because it gets put together in such a different way than a print comic," continues Brown. "Gerry would give me a few things that he wanted to make sure got touched upon, but since I was the one with the most experience doing digital comics, he really gave me a lot of freedom."

With great freedom came great responsibility, as Brown soon discovered. "When working on one of the Infinite Comics, the storyboarding phase becomes a much bigger task than in a regular print comic," he says. "There are more moving parts to take into account, and when you deal with things like the screen scrolling, overlaying panels on top of each other, or changing artwork that's already visible, there are a lot more opportunities to do some really fun storytelling. Also, the layout itself becomes a much bigger part of the actual storytelling, so getting the layout right is a much more crucial process. Because of this, the writers I work with tend to give me a lot of freedom to control the story, which is why I usually get credited with cowriter or coplotter when I do storyboards."

Running parallel to Deadpool's regular ongoing series, *Deadpool: The Gauntlet* introduced a major character to the Merc with a Mouth's life: Dracula's intended wife, Shiklah. In the story, Dracula hired Deadpool to bring Shiklah to him, but as Wade got to know this monster queen, he quickly fell in love with her. By the end of the series, the two got married, leading to a battle with Dracula's minions and the famous vampire himself.

The task of designing Deadpool's beautiful bride fell to Reilly Brown. "I wanted her to look seductive and vampiric, but at the same time look like a super hero, so she has the tights and the bright colors and the cape," says Brown. "Her design was largely influenced by characters like the Scarlet Witch or Poison Ivy, who wear bathing suits with stockings." Brown also threw in a bit of contemporary fashion sense for good measure: "I'd been noticing a lot of women wearing patterned clothes at the time, so with Shiklah I came up with a lacy skull pattern to put on the stockings to make her look a bit more stylish and unique. It was hard to get that skull pattern right, so that it would be easy to apply to the art but wouldn't look too repetitive, so I had to have the skulls arranged at just the right angle that they'd always look right."

OPPOSITE AND BELOW Reilly Brown was able to play with pacing and composition in entirely new ways when constructing the first digital Deadpool Infinite Comic. [Art by Reilly Brown from *Deadpool: The Gauntlet* #3, January 2014]

A key element of Shiklah's character is her ability to transform into a literal monster, a hulking beast that would frighten away any sane suitor. Obviously, she was perfect for Deadpool. "Because we were doing the comic digitally, I really wanted her to have shape-shifting powers, because I thought that would work really well with the digital format," says Brown. "I wanted her true monster form to be recognizably female, but truly scary and inhuman, so I gave her this big, scaly, spiky form, that was the opposite of her normal thin, elegant form. I thought [that] was a fun combination for her."

By the end of *Deadpool: The Gauntlet*, Shiklah and Wade were married, but the ceremony was saved for Deadpool's ongoing print title. In issue #27 (June 2014), drawn by the main artist on the book, Mike Hawthorne, the two were married in grand style with a huge crowd of famous attendees, and X-Man Nightcrawler officiating. While the event took many by surprise, Reilly Brown knew from the beginning that Shiklah was going to be Mrs. Deadpool. "That was something that I kept in mind when I designed her," he says. "I gave her the eye makeup so that it would go along with his mask, in a way, and the idea that her pretty face was a mask for a more monstrous form was similar to how he wears a mask to cover up his own true face."

Deadpool soon grew accustomed to married life as his ongoing series continued up to issue #45 (June 2015), billed as his 250th official issue, with art by penciller Mike Hawthorne and his inker Terry Pallot, as well as series regular artists Salva Espin and John Lucas. However, before this volume ended, Wade located his daughter Eleanor and saw her placed in Agent Preston's home. He kept a watchful eye on the family, even bonding with Ellie from time to time. But in the end, it all proved for naught as the events of the epic Marvel crossover event *Secret Wars* seemed to wipe Deadpool and all of his supporting cast from the face of the Earth, bringing this volume of Deadpool's comic to a close in its wake.

But, as any long term Deadpool fan knows, it takes more than a cosmic event to keep the Merc with a Mouth down. In January 2016, a fourth Deadpool ongoing series debuted, handled by the familiar team of Gerry Duggan, Mike Hawthorne, and Terry Pallot. Now a member of the Avengers in the brave new world of the reformed Marvel Universe, this series followed Deadpool as he formed a "Heroes for Hire" business—later changing the name to "Mercs for Money" to avoid a legal challenge from Luke Cage, who first established the Heroes for Hire name. Mercs for Money employed several obscure faces from Marvel's past—lackeys willing to take any odd job, from crime fighting to entertaining at bar mitzvahs. This band of rogues would even get their own title in April 2016, with *Deadpool: The Mercs For Money*, by writer Cullen Bunn and artist Salva Espin. It seemed Deadpool was truly trying to make up for a lifetime of wrongdoing, but, true to his character, becoming a hero would not be an easy undertaking.

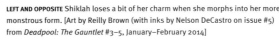
LEFT AND OPPOSITE Shiklah loses a bit of her charm when she morphs into her more monstrous form. [Art by Reilly Brown (with inks by Nelson DeCastro on issue #5) from *Deadpool: The Gauntlet* #3–5, January–February 2014]

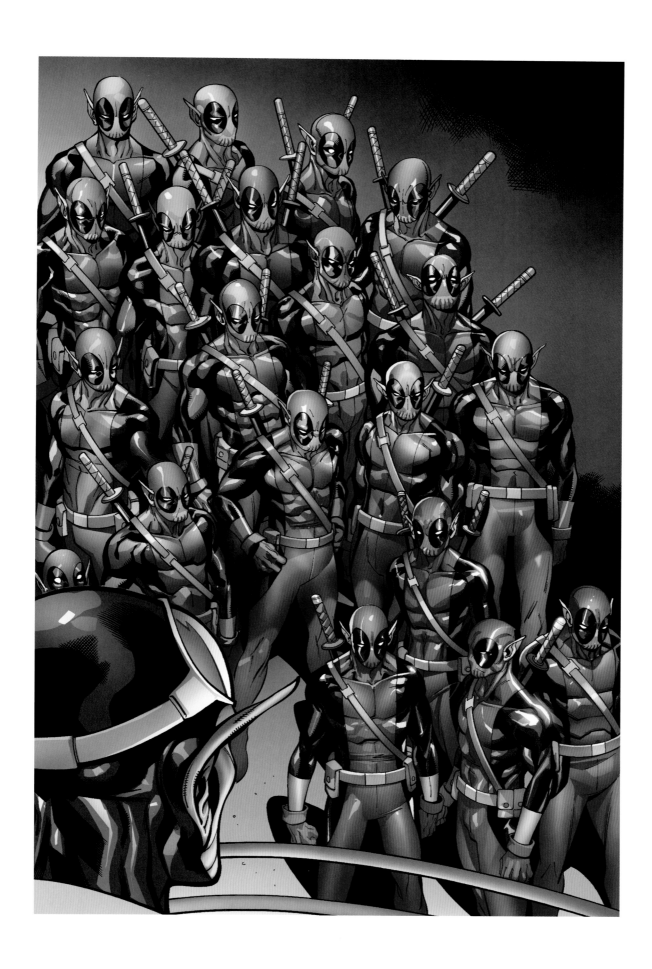

OPPOSITE Deadpool proves himself the Mascot with a Mouth when going undercover to battle the Skrulls. [Pencils by Paco Medina; inks by Juan Vlasco from *Deadpool* (Vol. 2) #1, November 2008]

ABOVE When you make a copy of a copy, expect the worst. The Skrulls find this out the hard way when they attempt to make their own Deadpool army. [Pencils by Paco Medina; inks by Juan Vlasco from *Deadpool* (Vol. 2) #2, November 2008]

THESE PAGES Artist Jason Pearson supplies a memorable series of covers for Deadpool's second ongoing series, perfectly capturing the relationship between Deadpool and his former associate Bullseye (shown here masquerading as the hero Hawkeye). [Art by Jason Pearson from *Deadpool* (Vol. 2) #6 and #10–12, March and July–September 2009]

ABOVE LEFT AND ABOVE RIGHT Just because his title was restarted for a new era doesn't mean Deadpool would abandon parodies. Issue #7 of his new series saw a homage to the classic cover from the seminal X-Men storyline "Days of Future Past." [Pencils by John Byrne; inks by Terry Austin from *The Uncanny X-Men* #141, January 1981 / Art by Jason Pearson from *Deadpool* (Vol. 2) #7, April 2009]

OPPOSITE Deadpool contemplates whether the pirate life is indeed for him. [Cover art by Jason Pearson from *Deadpool* (Vol. 2) #14, October 2009]

OPPOSITE AND ABOVE This sequence featuring an unfortunate pizza delivery guy later inspired a scene in Deadpool's first feature film. [Pencils by Paco Medina; inks by Juan Vlasco from *Deadpool* (Vol. 2) #10, July 2009]

OPPOSITE Despite his attempts, Deadpool just can't seem to fit in with the X-Men. And when you can't fit in with a band of social outcasts, that's certainly saying something. [Cover art by Jason Pearson from *Deadpool* (Vol. 2) #16 and #17, December 2009 and January 2010]

ABOVE LEFT Just a normal day at the office for the Merc with a Mouth. [Cover art by Dave Johnson from *Deadpool* (Vol. 2) #35, June 2011]

ABOVE RIGHT Deadpool isn't half as deadly as Evil Deadpool. I mean come on, it's right there in the name! [Cover art by Nick Bradshaw from *Deadpool* (Vol. 2) #45, December 2011]

ABOVE Wade Wilson is as much of a pain in the posterior for the Hulk as the cactus spines are for him. [Pencils by Bong Dazo; inks by Joe Pimental from *Deadpool* (Vol. 2) #37, July 2011]

OPPOSITE Unfortunately for Deadpool, green means go. [Cover art by Dave Johnson from *Deadpool* (Vol. 2) #39, August 2011]

OPPOSITE A face you can trust—scout's honor. [Cover art by Mark Brooks from *Deadpool* (Vol. 3) #22, March 2014]

ABOVE LEFT During the celebration of his twenty-fifth issue, Deadpool is unafraid to toot his own horn. [Cover art by Mark Brooks from *Deadpool* (Vol. 3) #25, May 2014]

ABOVE RIGHT While the rest of Marvel participates in the AXIS crossover event, Deadpool takes the opportunity to recharge his own batteries, unlike his cover costar Iron Man. [Art by David Nakayama from *Deadpool* (Vol. 3) #36, December 2014]

ABOVE What's creepier than the *Alien* movie franchise? Deadpool doing his best
impression of the *Alien* movie franchise. [Cover art by Mark Brooks from *Deadpool*
(Vol. 3) #23, April 2014]

OPPOSITE Madpool? Deadpool stars in a cover that parodies the *Mad Max* movies.
[Art by Mark Brooks from *Deadpool* (Vol. 3) #41, March 2015]

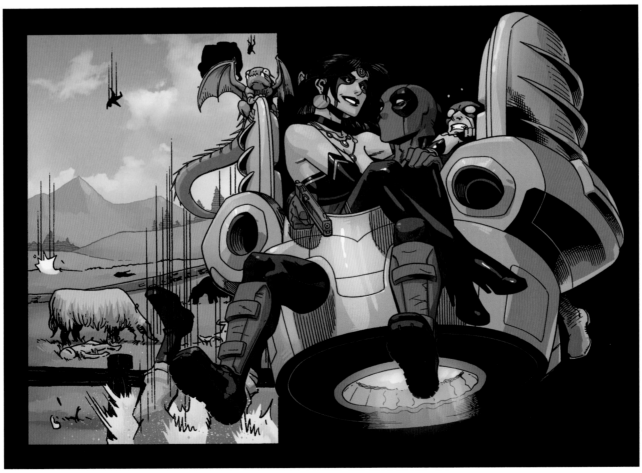

OPPOSITE TOP Deadpool's first Infinite Comic starts with a bang as he rescues a young lady, only to be shunned by her when she catches a glimpse of his unmasked face. [Art by Reilly Brown from *Deadpool: The Gauntlet* #1, January 2014).]

OPPOSITE BOTTOM Deadpool takes way too many liberties with M.O.D.O.K.'s chair after defeating the infamous villain. [Pencils by Reilly Brown; inks by Nelson DeCastro and Terry Pallot from *Deadpool: The Gauntlet* #7, February 2014]

ABOVE No humor is off-limits for Deadpool—bathroom, bedroom, or otherwise. [Storyboards by Reilly Brown; art by Khary Randolph from *Deadpool: The Gauntlet* #7, February 2014]

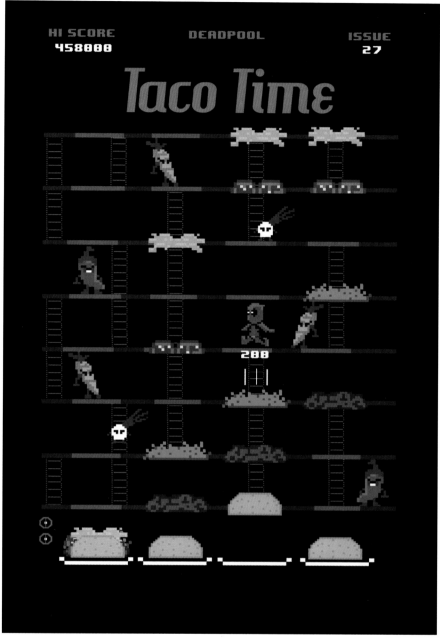

TO THE MAX

In December of 2010, Deadpool's violence and humor were taken to the next level when given the MAX treatment. The Marvel Comics' imprint dubbed MAX was intended only for mature readers and seemed a perfect fit for Wade Wilson, giving the title's creators a chance to amp up the violence, cursing, and even nudity.

The first *Deadpool MAX* series lasted twelve issues. It was written by David Lapham, famous for his work on the cult hit *Stray Bullets* as well as mainstream titles like *Detective Comics*. The series was drawn by legendary cartoonist Kyle Baker, who made waves on *The Shadow* before writing and drawing several highly successful and influential graphic novels, including *Why I Hate Saturn*. *Deadpool MAX* proved a success, and a six-issue sequel by the same creative team debuted in 2011, followed by a Christmas special in 2012.

THESE PAGES Renowned artist Kyle Baker proves himself right at home in a mature readers' title. [Cover art by Kyle Baker from *Deadpool MAX* #4 and #7, March and June 2011, and *Deadpool MAX II* #4 and #5, March and April 2012]

OPPOSITE Hostess cakes ads starring super heroes were a staple of comics in the 1970s and '80s, a tradition ripe for parody in this faux Deadpool ad for Party Time Fruit Liquor. [Art by Scott Koblish from *Deadpool* (Vol. 3) # 7, June 2013]

ABOVE Gerry Duggan and Brian Posehn's flashback issues of *Deadpool* are made all the more brilliant thanks to artwork designed to match the comics of the time period in which the stories take place. [Art by Scott Koblish from *Deadpool* (Vol. 3) #13, September 2013]

FOLLOWING PAGES When Deadpool faced the menace of the corrupt Roxxon corporation, his comic book was transformed into a faux coloring book. [Art by Scott Koblish from *Deadpool* (Vol. 3) #40, March 2015]

OPPOSITE Age ain't nothing but a number. The final issue of Deadpool's third ongoing series is celebrated as the mercenary hits his 250th issue. [Cover art by Scott Koblish from *Deadpool* (Vol. 3) #45, June 2015]

ABOVE Most mercenaries don't find themselves in space fighting an undead Ronald Reagan. Lucky for readers, Deadpool isn't your average killer for hire. [Cover art by Geof Darrow from *Deadpool* (Vol. 3) #5, April 2013]

ABOVE X-Man Nightcrawler officiates at the wedding of the century as Shiklah and Deadpool tie the knot. [Art by Mike Hawthorne from *Deadpool* (Vol. 3) #27, June 2014]

OPPOSITE Deadpool set a Guinness World Record for the number of characters on a single comic book cover when Wade Wilson and Shiklah were wed. [Art by Scott Koblish from *Deadpool* (Vol. 3) #27, June 2014]

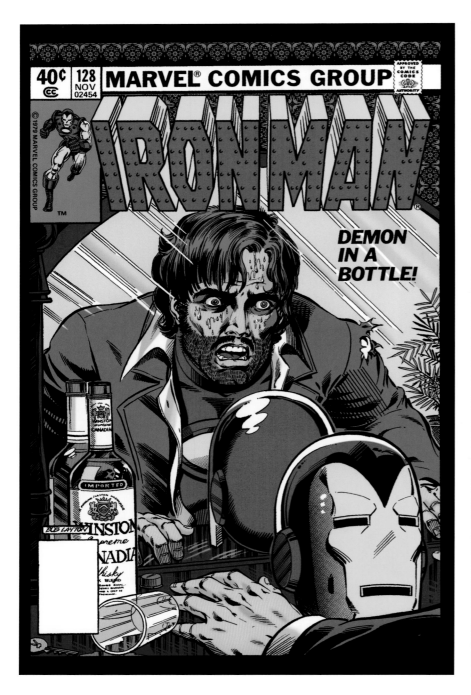

ABOVE LEFT AND ABOVE RIGHT Tony Stark suffers from Deadpoolism in a cover that parodies the famous *Iron Man* "Demon in a Bottle" storyline. [Art by Bob Layton from *Iron Man* #128, November 1979 / Art by Kevin Maguire from *Deadpool* (Vol. 3) #7, June 2013]

OPPOSITE Batman's first appearance on the cover of *Detective Comics* #27 (May 1939) also gets its own send-up by the Merc with a Mouth. [Art by Arthur Adams from *Deadpool* (Vol. 3) #27, June 2014]

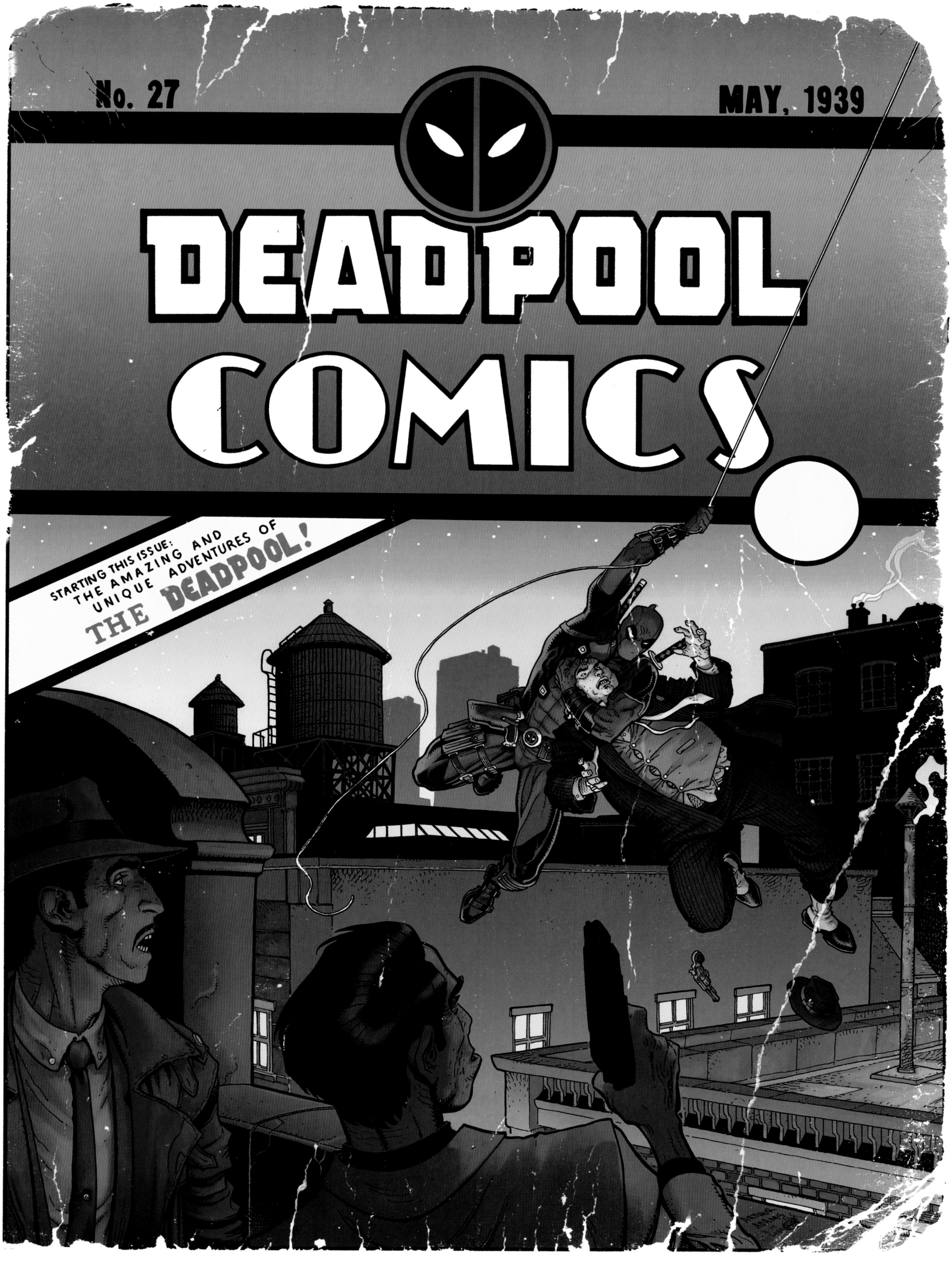
No. 27
MAY, 1939
DEADPOOL COMICS
STARTING THIS ISSUE: THE AMAZING AND UNIQUE ADVENTURES OF THE DEADPOOL!

OPPOSITE When going into business with a few associates from Marvel's storied history, Deadpool opts to color-code his employees. [Cover art by Mike Hawthorne from *Deadpool* (Vol. 4) #4, February 2016]

ABOVE In the 1990s, Marvel experimented with several titles set in the future year of 2099. It took Deadpool a while to catch up with the trend. [Cover art by Scott Koblish from *Deadpool* (Vol. 4) #6, March 2016]

CHAPTER 7
DEADPOOL'S WORLD

Since the beginning of his career, Deadpool has been a character nearly impossible to rein in. The more he appeared in *X-Force* and in his own miniseries, the more he began to pop up in other Marvel titles. A prolific guest star whose sheer number of cameos rivals that of characters like Spider-Man, Wolverine, and the Punisher, Deadpool has also appeared in a number of spin-off series, encompassing both limited and ongoing formats. To this day, Deadpool continues to grow in popularity, making it clear that this is Deadpool's world, and we're only living in it.

As early as September 1993, Deadpool began making appearances in other titles while also starring in his own series. While enjoying his first miniseries, the Merc with a Mouth found time to make an appearance in *Avengers* #366. In 1994, not only did Deadpool show up for a bout with Logan in issue # 88 of Wolverine's first ongoing series (December 1994), but he also served briefly in the ever-changing team known as the Secret Defenders. The idea of Deadpool being a team player seemed preposterous at the time, considering his shaky reputation, and for a while, Wade Wilson limited his team exposure to brief appearances in *X-Force*, *Silver Sable & the Wild Pack*, and *Heroes for Hire*. But by 2007, Deadpool opted to spend an entire special hanging out with the Great Lakes Avengers in Deadpool/ GLI: Summer Fun Spectacular.

With so many team-ups under his belt, the Merc with a Mouth was perhaps ready to join a super-hero team. But when he was unable to find a team that would have him, Deadpool opted to go out and form one of his own. *Deadpool Corps*, an ongoing title starring Deadpool and a band of alternate-reality Deadpools, debuted in June 2010, but the seeds for this twelve-issue ongoing title were planted far earlier. Marvel Comics had long ago strayed into other dimensions— varied realities that contained vastly different status quos for Marvel's iconic cast of characters. In one of those worlds, as seen in the miniseries *Marvel Zombies*, a zombie virus had turned some of the most famous super heroes and villains into undead walking corpses. Deadpool was included in that number, but, because all that was left of him was a severed zombie head, he wasn't walking anywhere. He was still able to wisecrack, though, when not trying to feed on the brains of others.

This Deadpool—who would later become known as Headpool—ventured into the main Marvel Universe in the pages of another new title, the thirteen-issue *Deadpool: Merc with a Mouth* series. The series began in September of 2009, with writer Victor Gischler at the helm, navigating increasingly ridiculous and often choppy waters with the help of artists Bong Dazo and Jose Pimentel. The plot saw several parties all try to get their hands on Headpool—who was considered a bioweapon of mass destruction—including the regular universe's Deadpool, the terrorist organiza- tion A.I.M., love interest Dr. Betty Swanson, and even new sidekick Bill, Agent of A.I.M.

In issue #7, Gischler and Dazo introduced a Deadpool from another parallel universe named Lady Deadpool. A female Merc with a Mouth just as deadly as her male counterpart, Lady Deadpool played a role in Wade Wilson's life

OPPOSITE Don't go in the water. Deadpool and Headpool parody the original *Jaws* movie poster. [Cover art by Arthur Suydam from *Deadpool: Merc with a Mouth* #2, October 2009]

that would increase considerably by issue #13, the final comic of that series. In that issue, a powerful cosmic entity known as the Contemplator would recruit Deadpool to form his own team of vigilantes in order to battle the cosmic threat of a being called the Cosmic Awareness.

Gischler's next stop was penning the five-issue *Prelude to Deadpool Corps*, which established just who would be on the roster of Wilson's team: Lady Deadpool, Headpool, a child named Kidpool, and even a canine version of Deadpool called Dogpool. This miniseries led directly into *Deadpool Corps*, which saw Gischler partnered with Deadpool's co-creator Rob Liefeld on pencils, with inks by Adelso Corona.

While the Deadpool Corps did save the universe, they also outwore their welcome with the Contemplator quickly enough and were soon sent back to their respective dimensions. This was probably just as well for Deadpool, as he'd somehow found his way onto a respectable team in the meantime in the pages of ongoing series *Uncanny X-Force*, which debuted in December 2010.

Marvel superstar writer Rick Remender supplied the scripts for the thirty-five-issue series of *Uncanny X-Force*, with artist Jerome Opeña originally handling the art chores before many other artists came onboard for later issues and arcs. The series showed Wade sporting a spiffy new white-and-black costume, and featured other team members well known to X-Men fans including Wolverine, Angel, Fantomex, and Psylocke. It was also notable for establishing the paternal relationship between Deadpool and a young mutant named Evan, who was actually the longtime X-Men foe Apocalypse, reincarnated into the form of an innocent boy.

Near the conclusion of Deadpool's tenure on the Uncanny X-Force, a very different kind of Deadpool was causing trouble in another dimension of Marvel's multiverse. In *Deadpool Kills the Marvel Universe*, featuring twisted writing by Cullen Bunn and equally violent artwork from Dalibor Talajic, the Merc with a Mouth's insanity was fully unleashed as he murdered nearly every famous face on Marvel's roster. The series would prove popular enough that it soon spawned a sequel, *Deadpool Killustrated*, a parody of the old Classics Illustrated comics that retold famous tales from literature in comic book form. In this four-issue series by Bunn, penciller Matteo Lolli, and inker Sean Parsons, the same alternate-universe Deadpool who killed the Marvel Universe characters traveled to the Ideaverse—another universe where famous literary tales originated—to brutally murder heroes and heroines from classic novels. This unstable Deadpool would later discover the existence of the regular Deadpool, clashing with his other-dimensional equivalent in another four-issue tale, appropriately titled *Deadpool Kills Deadpool*. This series by Bunn and artist Salva Espin saw all of Deadpool's former partners from the Deadpool Corps killed by the rogue Deadpool, before the villain was bested.

In February of 2013, Deadpool found time to appear in another team book, *Thunderbolts*, once again reunited with writer Daniel Way, with art handled by Steve Dillon. The creative team shifted several times on the title, with various artists and writers trying their hand. The Thunderbolts fell apart by issue #32 (December 2014), and the members of the team all went their separate ways. With a cleared slate and a hankering to bring chaos to another team of do-gooders, Deadpool unwittingly wandered into the big time when he was chosen by Steve Rogers, aka Captain America, to join the Avengers. In the pages of 2015's *Uncanny Avengers*, Deadpool began his service in the Avengers Unity Squad. Written by Gerry Duggan and drawn by Ryan Stegman, *Uncanny Avengers* saw Deadpool try to turn over a new leaf as he not only served as a member of Rogers' team, but also helped pay their bills by selling his own popular merchandise. Deadpool's membership didn't sit well with all his fellow Avengers, however, and issue #1 of the title saw Spider-Man quit the team out of protest.

Everyone's favorite web-slinger wouldn't be able to get away from Deadpool that easily, however, as March 2016 saw the birth of a new ongoing team-up title, *Spider-Man/Deadpool,* as the two unlikely allies began to work together at Deadpool's insistence and much to Peter Parker's chagrin. The book was created by familiar Deadpool experts, writer Joe Kelly and penciller Ed McGuinness, and was inked by Mark Morales. Kelly's return to Deadpool on an ongoing title was highly anticipated by fans, and one he expects to be his last: "I'd never say never, but generally I don't go back to characters that I've had a long run on. It's not a personal code or anything, just always looking for new and exciting territory to play in."

Kelly also seems to believe Deadpool is in capable hands in the pages of his own monthly book. "Gerry Duggan's run has been awesome," says Kelly, an opinion shared by another Deadpool alum, Mark Waid. Says Waid, "Gerry Duggan has that character down cold, as far as I'm concerned." If Deadpool's current popularity is any indication, the fans agree.

THESE PAGES Apparently Deadpool is among those who don't appreciate the nuanced art form known as mime in this stylized wraparound cover that evokes the type of imagery found in the opening sequences of James Bond films. [Art by Dave Johnson from *Deadpool* #900, December 2009]

OPPOSITE On this variant cover that parodies the marriage between Peter Parker and Mary Jane Watson, Deadpool takes it upon himself to kiss the bride. [Art by Pasqual Ferry from *The Amazing Spider-Man* #620, April 2010]

ABOVE In one of his earliest adventures, Deadpool mixes it up with the Avengers' Black Knight. [Pencils by Mike Gustovich; inks by Ariane Lenshoek from *Avengers* #366, September 1993]

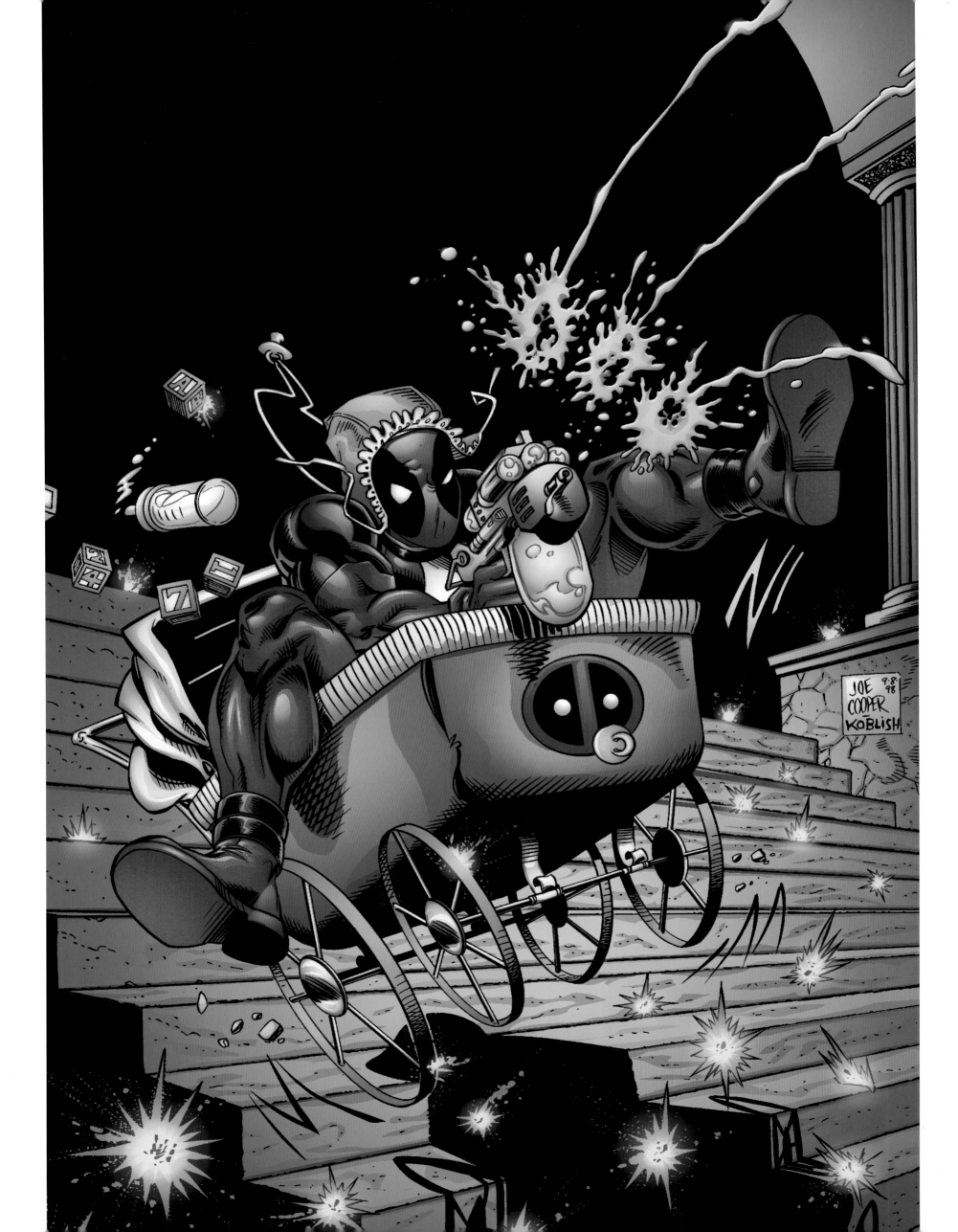

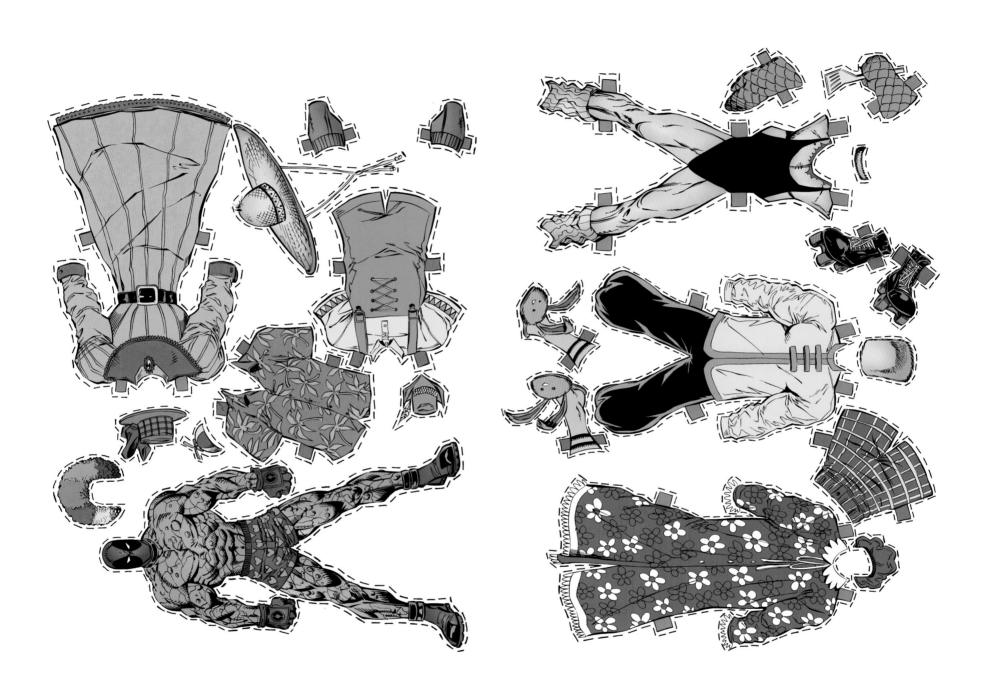

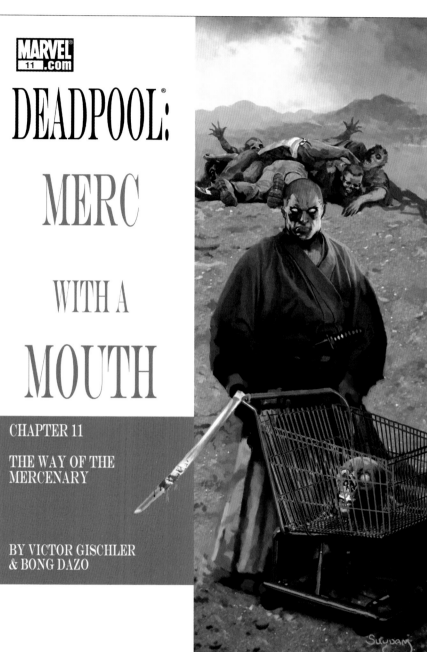

OPPOSITE It's Deadpool vs. Headpool in a cover that pays homage to Marvel's *Savage Tales* #1 (May 1971). [Art by Arthur Suydam from *Deadpool: Merc with a Mouth* #1, September 2009]

ABOVE LEFT Deadpool plays football with Headpool—one of the deadliest pigskins there is—on this variant cover. [Art by Ed McGuinness from *Deadpool: Merc with a Mouth* #1, September 2009]

ABOVE RIGHT Wade Wilson goes on a shopping spree from hell in this cover inspired by the beloved Japanese comic *Lone Wolf and Cub*. [Art by Arthur Suydam from *Deadpool: Merc with a Mouth* #11, July 2010]

TEAM-UPS IN THE BLOOD

Deadpool has a long history of playing the foil to otherwise more serious characters, a team-up tradition that began with the original *Cable & Deadpool* series of 2004. This tradition was further explored in 2010 with the arrival of the *Deadpool Team-Up* title. The book was preceded by a spoof issue of sorts, Deadpool #900. With DC Comics' Superman on the verge of reaching his 900th issue of Action Comics, it was decided that the Merc with a Mouth should reach this milestone before the Man of Steel, despite the fact that he was nowhere near having that many issues under his belt. After issue #900, Marvel kept the momentum going, counting down the next month with *Deadpool Team-Up* #899, followed by #898 and so on. The title saw Wade Wilson join forces with the likes of Thor, Hercules, and even Galactus—the latter team-up seeing Deadpool struggling to survive after becoming the godlike figure's cosmic herald.

Another team-up opportunity presented itself with 2015's *Deadpool & Cable: Split Second*, a further digital release from the Infinite Comics imprint. This miniseries not only reunited the famous odd couple, but it also served as a reunion for Deadpool veterans Fabian Nicieza and Reilly Brown. Unlike the stars of their comic collaboration, Nicieza and Brown seemed to get along swimmingly. "I always have a great time working with Fabian," says Brown. "There's always a lot of back and forth over the phone, or over beers, brainstorming and coming up with gags or cool moments to include. With him it's always a true collaboration, which is a lot of fun, and always very energizing."

"Reilly's skill set at understanding the possibilities, potential, and even limitations of the current digital process means he gets to drive the car when it came to breaking down our story," says Nicieza. "We coplotted the book in true fashion, talking the story out, then I would break down a tight outline of the individual chapter scenes, but he would break all of that down into the component pages and panel flow. This meant Reilly was determining all the storytelling beats, which included generating a lot of the visual humor and coming up with entire 'bits.'"

One of these "bits" was the reverse-time storytelling aspect of a story that would see Deadpool clash with a time-hopping future version of himself called Loop and which could be read in two directions to tell two slightly different stories. While the result was particularly satisfying, it was a bear to execute. "There was this one issue in particular where I had this crazy idea that while Deadpool was traveling forward in time, he'd encounter another version of himself that was traveling backward in time, so when you get to the end of the issue, you can just turn around and read it all backward, creating a perfect time loop," says Brown. "By the end, after talking for hours and hours about what works and doesn't work with time travel, and Deadpool, and reading comics backward, Fabian was about ready to kill me! I think it all worked out pretty well in the end, and it was a fun experiment."

OPPOSITE Deadpool's team-up title doesn't quite cut the mustard when it's canceled alongside *Deadpool Corps*. [Cover art by Skottie Young from *Deadpool Team-Up* #883, May 2011]

BOTTOM FAR LEFT Deadpool has been aware of his readers watching him for quite some time, but the Watcher is another matter altogether. [Cover art by Skottie Young from *Deadpool Team-Up* #884, April 2011]

BOTTOM CENTER LEFT Caught between a rock and a hard place. [Cover art by Humberto Ramos from *Deadpool Team-Up* #888, December 2010]

BOTTOM CENTER RIGHT Deadpool's not quite worthy to wield the hammer of Thor. [Cover art by Humberto Ramos from *Deadpool Team-Up* #887, January 2011]

BOTTOM FAR RIGHT True sons of anarchy: Deadpool and the Ghost Riders. [Cover art by Humberto Ramos from *Deadpool Team-Up* #897, March 2010]

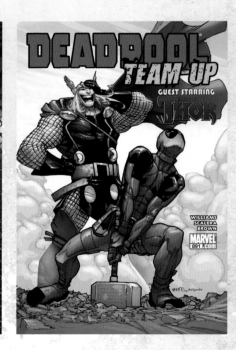

ABOVE Deadpool hits issue #1000 (except not really) in this one-shot special. [Cover art by Dave Johnson from *Deadpool* #1000, October 2010]

OPPOSITE The Man Without Fear finds Deadpool as irritating as a pitchfork on a chalkboard in this variant cover that parodies the memorable cover for *Daredevil* #187 (October 1982) by legendary creators Frank Miller and Klaus Janson. The cover is exactly the same as the original except for the inclusion of Deadpool. [Art by Max Fiumara from *Daredevil* #505, April 2010]

M
DAREDEVIL
...!
STOP IT! PLEASE...
...STOP IT...
ANNOYING FRANK MILLER
REYNOLD'S WRAP
ALUMINUIM FOIL

OPPOSITE TOP LEFT To celebrate its seventieth anniversary, Marvel released a series of variant "frame" covers depicting many of its iconic characters. [Art by Tony Moore and Jim Cheung from *Deadpool: Merc with a Mouth* #2, October 2009]

OPPOSITE AND ABOVE While the covers had little to do with the interiors, *Deadpool: Merc with a Mouth* enjoyed poking fun at a variety of iconic movie posters, including *Dawn of the Dead* (**OPPOSITE TOP RIGHT**), *Scarface* (**OPPOSITE BOTTOM LEFT**), *Pretty Woman* (**OPPOSITE BOTTOM RIGHT**), *Trainspotting* (**ABOVE LEFT**), and *The Graduate* (**ABOVE RIGHT**). [Art by Arthur Suydam from *Deadpool: Merc with a Mouth* #3–5, 7, and 9, November 2009, January 2010, March 2010, and May 2010]

OPPOSITE No medium is off-limits for artist Arthur Suydam, not even the cover to Nirvana's famous album *Nevermind*. [Cover art by Arthur Suydam from *Deadpool: Merc with a Mouth* #12, August 2010]

ABOVE The final issue of *Merc with a Mouth* features a parody cover inspired by the movie poster for *The Silence of the Lambs*. [Art by Arthur Suydam from *Deadpool: Merc with a Mouth* #13, September 2010]

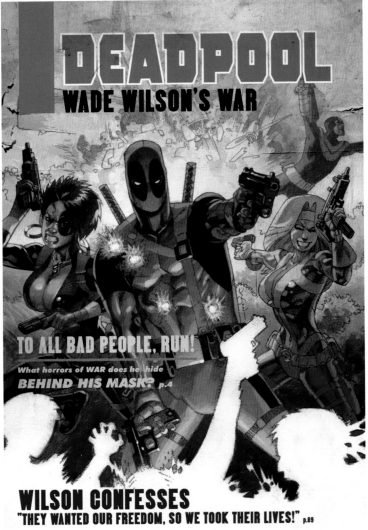

OPPOSITE LEFT Not content with simply starring in a monthly title or two, Deadpool also inspired a handful of miniseries, including *Deadpool: Suicide Kings*. [Cover art by Mike McKone from *Deadpool: Suicide Kings* #1, June 2009]

OPPOSITE RIGHT Deadpool makes a brief four-issue entry into the Marvel Knights imprint for a particularly colorful revenge fantasy storyline. [Cover art by Jason Pearson from *Deadpool: Wade Wilson's War* #1, August 2010]

ABOVE Deadpool kills an alternate reality version of himself, the Deadpool Kid, who apparently wasn't as quick on the draw as he believed. [Art by Das Pastoras from *Deadpool: Merc with a Mouth* #7, March 2010]

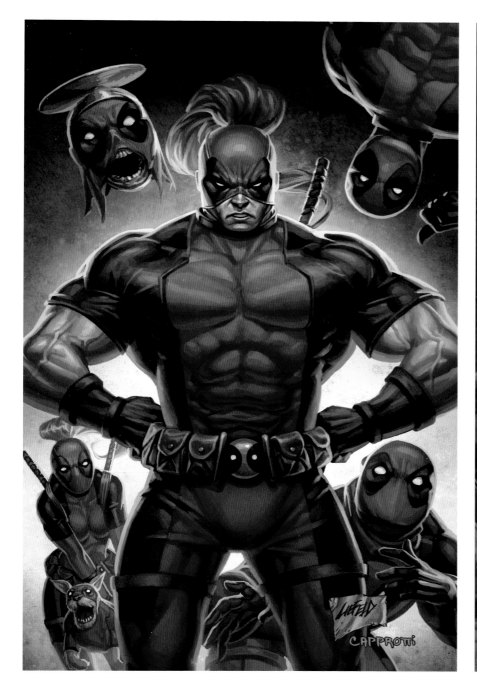

OPPOSITE AND ABOVE *Deadpool Corps* gave Rob Liefeld an excuse to draw covers that not only featured his famous co-creation but also several variations on the Merc with a Mouth, including Lady Deadpool, Headpool, Dogpool, and Kidpool. [Art by Rob Liefeld from *Deadpool Corps* #1–3, June–August 2010]

ABOVE LEFT Lady Deadpool makes her dramatic first appearance, celebrated on her own variant cover. [Art by Rob Liefeld from *Deadpool: Merc with a Mouth* #7, March 2010]

ABOVE RIGHT Wade Wilson begins a recruitment drive to seek out like-minded allies. Literally. [Cover art by Dave Johnson from *Prelude to Deadpool Corps* #1, May 2010]

OPPOSITE Deadpool's female counterpart proves popular enough to earn her own Women of Marvel one-shot. [Cover art by Greg Land from *Lady Deadpool* #1, September 2010]

ABOVE Deadpool and Lady Deadpool don't quite walk off into the sunset, but rather into another dimension, when the Merc with a Mouth recruits his female counterpart into a cosmic war. [Art by Rob Liefeld from *Prelude to Deadpool Corps* #1, May 2010]

OPPOSITE Each of the Deadpools is from his or her own reality—it's no wonder that the Deadpool Corps seems to get along swimmingly right from the start. [Pencils by Paco Medina; inks by Juan Vlasco from *Prelude to Deadpool Corps* #4, May 2010]

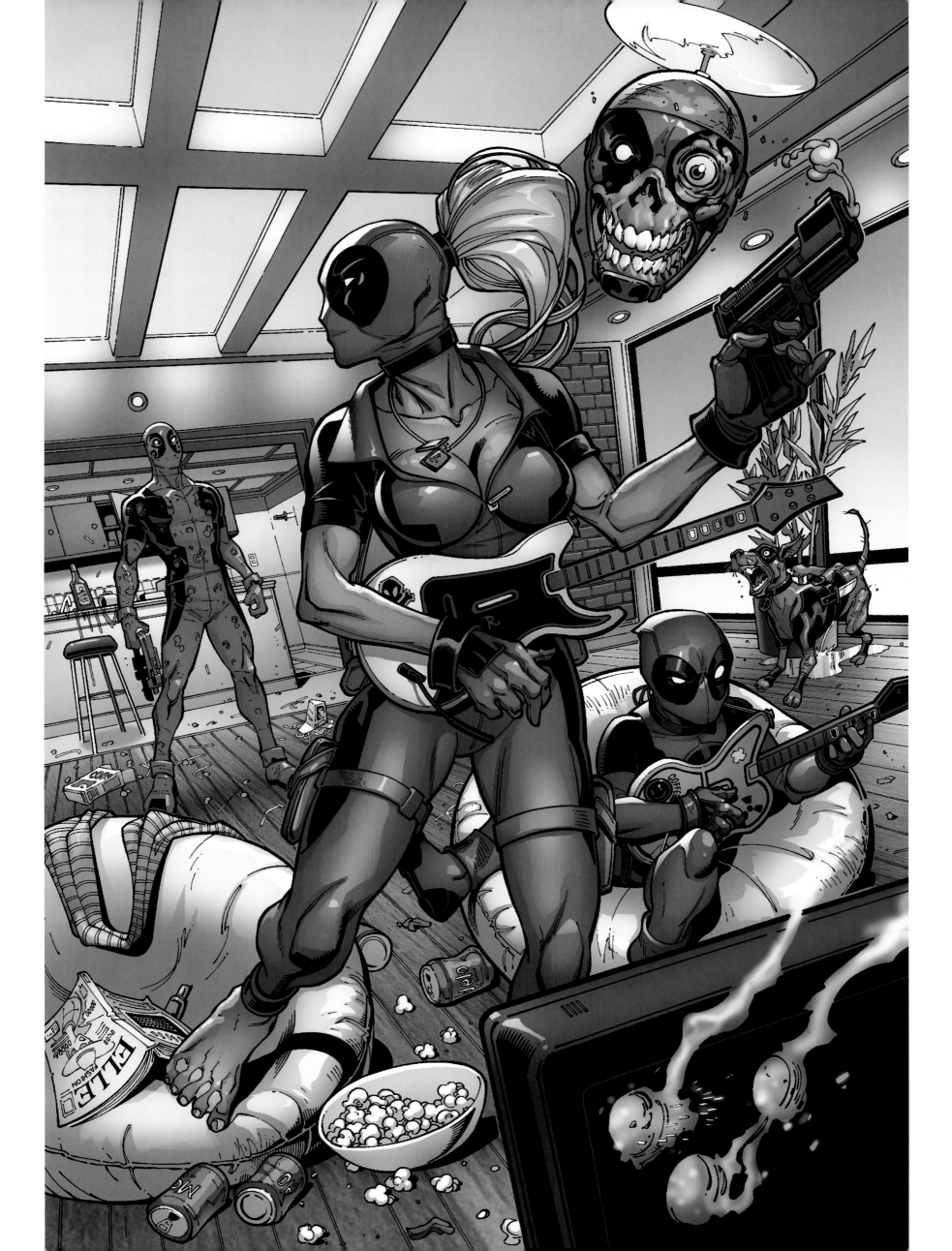

ABOVE AND OPPOSITE An alternate version of Deadpool stars in his very own pulp
miniseries, embracing the comic medium's noir roots. [Cover art by Jae Lee from
Deadpool: Pulp #1 and #2, November and December 2010]

OPPOSITE You're not fooling anyone, Wade. [Cover art by David Nakayama from *Deadpool* (Vol. 3) Annual #2, July 2014]

ABOVE LEFT AND ABOVE RIGHT The Merc with a Mouth seems a bit lost when he explodes onto the scene all by his lonesome in this variant cover that parodies the debut of one of the most famous incarnations of the X-Men. [Art by Giuseppe Camuncoli from *X-Men Legacy* #233, April 2010 / Art by Gil Kane and Dave Cockrum from *Giant-Size X-Men* #1, May 1975]

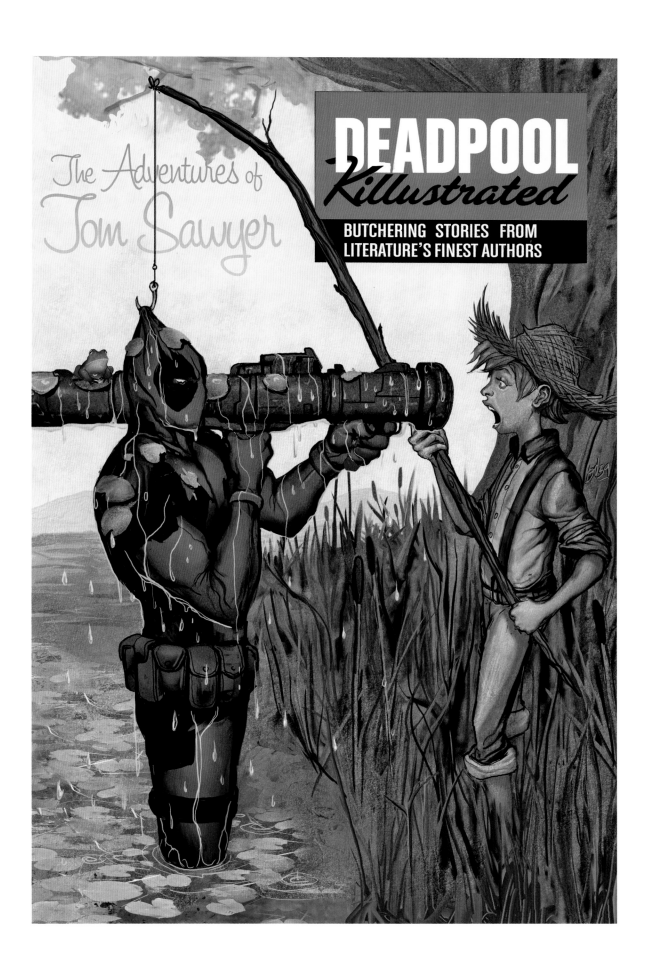

The Adventures of Tom Sawyer

DEADPOOL *Killustrated*

BUTCHERING STORIES FROM
LITERATURE'S FINEST AUTHORS

THESE AND FOLLOWING PAGES Deadpool makes short work of famous faces from literature,
including Moby-Dick, Tom Sawyer, Ebenezer Scrooge, and even Sherlock Holmes.
[Cover art by Mike Del Mundo from *Deadpool Killustrated* #1–4, March–June 2013]

ABOVE LEFT Deadpool is unleashed on his greatest killing spree to date. [Cover art by Kaare Andrews from *Deadpool Kills the Marvel Universe* #1, October 2012]

ABOVE RIGHT Everyone has a blind spot—for Deadpool, it's a hot, fresh chimichanga. [Cover art by Mike Del Mundo from *Deadpool Kills Deadpool* #2, October 2013]

OPPOSITE The killing finally comes to an end when the bloodthirsty alternate-universe Deadpool meets his match, thanks to the true Deadpool that fans know and love. [Cover art by Mike Del Mundo from *Deadpool Kills Deadpool* #4, December 2013]

FOLLOWING PAGES Everyone leaps into the 'Pool, no matter what dimension they are from. [Art by Salva Espin from *Deadpool Kills Deadpool* #2, October 2013]

ABOVE AND OPPOSITE After murdering Sun Tzu Wu, Deadpool attempts to publish his own
Art of War in this four-issue miniseries written by the incomparable Peter David. [Cover
art by Scott Koblish from *Deadpool's Art of War* #1–3, December 2014–February 2015]

OPPOSITE AND ABOVE In this four-issue miniseries, Deadpool discovers his world is overrun by zombies and gets busy doing what he does best. Hint: It involves a lot of killing. [Cover art by Jay Shaw from *Night of the Living Deadpool* #1–3, March–April 2014]

ABOVE The first meeting between Deadpool and Wolverine goes pretty much as expected. [Pencils by Adam Kubert; inks by Mark Farmer from *Wolverine* #88, December 1994]

OPPOSITE TOP LEFT One of Rob Liefeld's triumphant returns to Deadpool came when the plotter/artist opted to once again pit him against Wolverine. [Cover pencils by Rob Liefeld; inks by Norm Rapmund from *Wolverine* #154, September 2000]

OPPOSITE TOP RIGHT The Wolverine/Deadpool grudge match seemingly came to a close after their confrontation in this issue. However, when it comes to these two volatile characters, a truce doesn't last long. [Pencils by Walter McDaniel; inks by Scott Koblish and Walden Wong from *Wolverine '99 Annual*, December 1999]

OPPOSITE BOTTOM This powerful cover subtly hints at the Weapon X connection between Deadpool and Wolverine. [Art by Adam Kubert from *Wolverine* #88, December 1994]

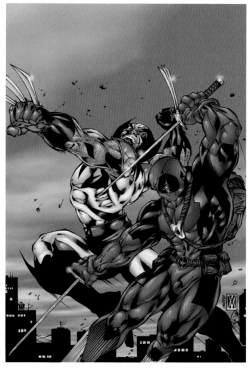

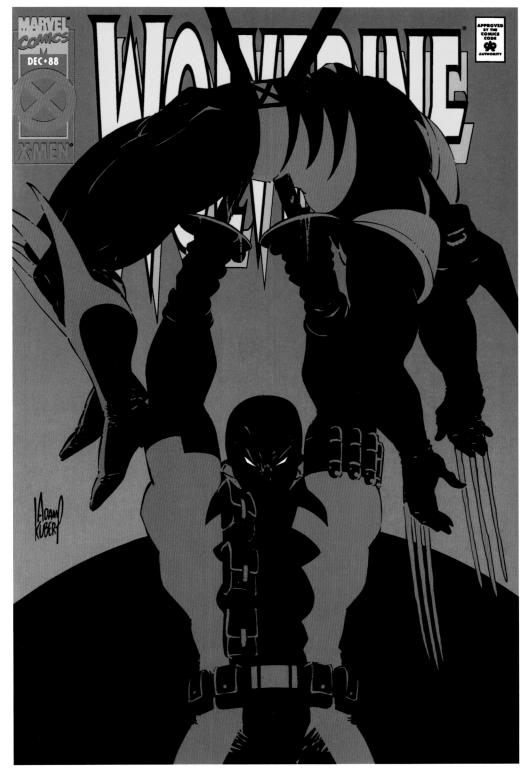

ABOVE LEFT Deadpool dons a new white costume to serve in the Uncanny X-Force. [Cover art by Esad Ribic from *Uncanny X-Force* #1, December 2010]

ABOVE RIGHT The original co-creator of X-Force, Rob Liefeld, handled one of the many variant issues that accompanied *Uncanny X-Force's* debut. [Art by Rob Liefeld from *Uncanny X-Force* #1, December 2010]

OPPOSITE The cover of the final issue of *Uncanny X-Force*, which ended its series with the final part of a massive eleven-part storyline entitled "The Final Execution Saga." [Art by Julian Totino Tedesco from *Uncanny X-Force* #35, February 2013]

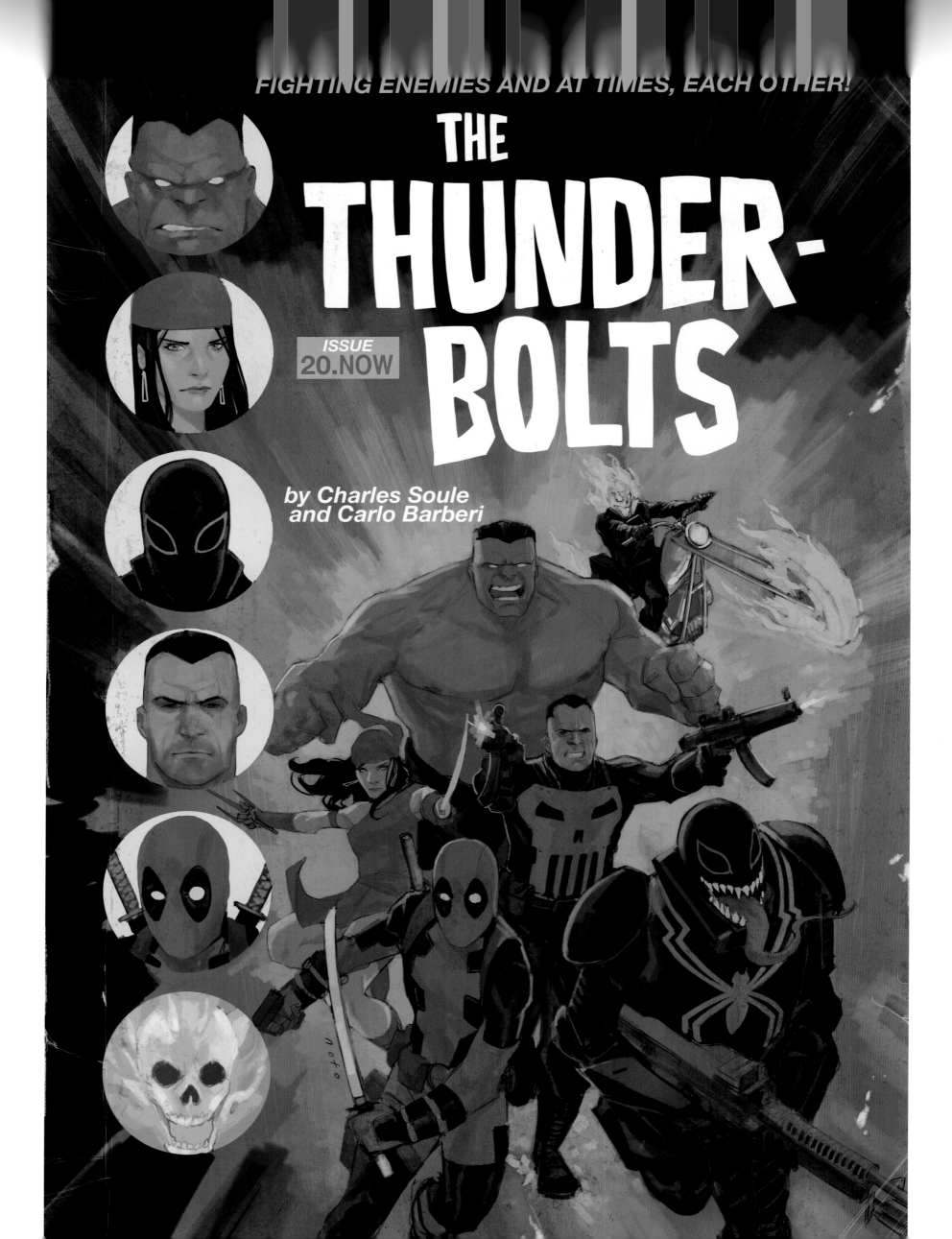

OPPOSITE Red Hulk, Elektra, Agent Venom, Punisher, Deadpool, and Ghost Rider: the perfect roster for the often morally ambiguous Thunderbolts. [Art by Phil Noto from *Thunderbolts* (Vol. 2) #20, March 2014]

ABOVE LEFT Cartoonist Skottie Young offered up a variety of Marvel NOW! variant covers, including this great spin on Deadpool's fledgling team, the Thunderbolts. [Art by Skottie Young from *Thunderbolts* (Vol. 2) #1, February 2013]

ABOVE RIGHT Katie Cook delivers a cuteness overload when she reimagines the Thunderbolts as a team of cats on this variant cover. [Art by Katie Cook from *Thunderbolts* (Vol. 2) #20, March 2014]

FOLLOWING PAGES Deadpool stands tall as an Avenger after finally being accepted by the masses as a hero. [Cover art by Ryan Stegman from *The Uncanny Avengers* (Vol. 3) #1]

CONCLUSION

*I*n a little over twenty-five years, Deadpool has made the difficult transition from third-tier villain to juggernaut franchise. He's gone from a cult favorite to iconic status and now ranks among those few dozen comic book characters recognizable to those that have never stepped foot inside a comic book store. He remains not just a fan favorite, but also a favorite among comic book creators.

"Deadpool's great because he's a character who you can do anything with," says Reilly Brown. "There's a lot of great visual humor you can do with the character that you can't get away with on other characters. You can twist him, tangle him, mangle him, dress him like a cheerleader, and it all works! But it's not always funny, and sometimes you get to make things serious, or even depressing. I love drawing characters where you get that full range of emotion."

"The character is me in that the unfiltered brain process that generates Deadpool's insanity was the *filtered* brain process that I endure every single day when interacting with society," says Fabian Nicieza. "So writing Deadpool is always fun because it's like monthly therapy without having to pay for a doctor."

"My favorite aspect of Deadpool has always boiled down to this," says Joe Kelly. "He is a character who wants to do good but is constitutionally incapable of doing so. On those rare occasions where he does step into the light, the universe kicks him in the stones. That's what makes him so relatable. Yes, he's funny. Yes, you get over-the-top action and the healing factor and all the super-shenanigans, but it's the fact that he wants so bad to be good and keeps screwing it up that makes us love him."

Love him for his fast mouth or love him for his impossible abilities, Deadpool is now a permanent addition to the Marvel landscape. His comics, movies, action figures, and T-shirts aren't going away anytime soon. It seems there is simply no getting rid of Deadpool. Ask any hero or villain in the Marvel Universe. Because they've certainly all tried . . .

OPPOSITE A new twist on the famous "Fastball Special" popularized by X-Men Colossus and Wolverine. This time around, it's Rogue doing the tossing. [Cover art by Ryan Stegman from *The Uncanny Avengers* (Vol. 3) #4, March 2016]

TITAN
BOOKS

144 Southwark Street
London SE1 0UP
www.titanbooks.com

Find us on Facebook: www.facebook.com/TitanBooks
Follow us on Twitter: @titanbooks

A CIP catalogue record for this title is available from the British Library.

ISBN: 9781785654282

Published by arrangement with
Insight Editions, PO Box 3088
San Rafael, CA 94912, USA.
www.insighteditions.com
Publisher: Raoul Goff
Acquisitions Manager: Robbie Schmidt
Art Director: Chrissy Kwasnik
Designer: Brie Brewer
Executive Editor: Vanessa Lopez
Senior Editor: Chris Prince
Production Editor: Elaine Ou
Associate Editor: Katie DeSandro
Production Managers: Alix Nicholaeff, Thomas Chung, and Lina sp Temena
Production Assistant: Jacob Frink and Sylvester Vang
Cover Illustration: Reilly Brown
Cover Color: Jim Charalampidis

Insight Editions would like to thank Curt Baker, Reilly Brown, Sarah Brunstad, David
Gabriel, Joseph Hochstein, Joe Kelly, Fabian Nicieza, Jeffrey Reingold, Mark Waid,
and Jeff Youngquist.

ROOTS of PEACE   REPLANTED PAPER

Insight Editions, in association with Roots of Peace, will plant two trees for each
tree used in the manufacturing of this book. Roots of Peace is an internationally
renowned humanitarian organization dedicated to eradicating land mines
worldwide and converting war-torn lands into productive farms and wildlife
habitats. Roots of Peace will plant two million fruit and nut trees in Afghanistan and
provide farmers there with the skills and support necessary for sustainable land
use.

Manufactured in China by Insight Editions

10 9 8 7 6 5 4 3 2 1